Teen secrets and letters

Authors & Compilers:

Tung Nguyen, Raheel Shah, Bar Segal,

Loell Wolfries and Ronald Baguma

Editor and Illustrator:

Loell Wolfries

Comic Consultants:

Bar Segal
Raheel Shah
Tung Nguyen

AuthorHouse™ UK Ltd.
500 Avebury Boulevard
Central Milton Keynes, MK9 2BE
www.authorhouse.co.uk
Phone: 08001974150

First published by AuthorHouse 1/27/2010

ISBN: 978-1-4490-8342-7 (sc)

This book is printed on acid-free paper.

authorHOUSE®

WELCOME!

Life can suck...

We will have friends we thought we could trust – only to find that they have broken our trust and backstabbed us.

We've had boyfriends or girlfriends that we thought loved us – only to find out that they might leave or hurt us in the end.

Try to find happiness through religion or education – only to find that they make us more lost and confused.

All the stories in this book are written by the modern day you and me; written by teenagers everywhere all over the world. It isn't written by an older person thinking back on his life, or some story teller thinking he can recreate what we as teenagers think and go through.

It is written by us... it's our stories... for us.

This book won't solve all your problems and it won't suddenly make you feel happy forever. It can certainly help you make better decisions and think positively, so that you can live a less painful and confused life.

Acknowledgement

We would like to thank all the contributors to this book, without them the book would not exist.

Thank you Kingston University, for supporting the work we put into this book, especially Yuliana Topazly, Debbie Anderson and David Stokes.

We would also like to thank family and friends that believed in us.

We dedicate this book to all the contributors
for their passion and integrity in composing
meaningful stories and poems for all to see.

We also dedicate this book to our readers.

One

One is born in a loving family, one is the eldest son, one lives in a big city, one studies in a school.

One breathes and sleeps and eats and one is bound to these actions without a physical choice.

One studies and works and socializes and one is bound to these actions without a mental choice.

One must set examples to other ones and one must reach the expectations of other ones.

One is given the role of a leader and one cannot turn it down.

One is to excel under any circumstances and one cannot fail.

One struggles and suffers, but one tells one-self that it is temporary.

Of course, one has the choice to give up and fail, but one was not taught like that, as one's choices are narrow and bound by his mind.

Of course, one can turn around and say no to everything that other ones care about and choose what one really wants for one-self, but one is not sure what one wants, because what one wants never existed.

One's wants and wills are placed into one's mind when one is born, and one only wants what one was taught to want.

One has feelings, and these feelings are what drive one to be.

One wants to be happy but the conventional methods to make one happy only leaves one content.

One seeks euphoria through unconventional methods but one is still left discontent.

One is deceived by the liberty that one is given, by the freedom of speech one has, by the important choices one must make, for these choices lead to further constraints and guilt in one's mind.

When one realizes one's lack of freedom; When one finds that one is one of the many; When one fails to impress with one's hard work; When one finally understands that one is the sum of other ones;

Yet does not succumb to this truth, and the suffering, the pain, the suffocation will lead one to become One.

By Zifeng Wei

Contents

Change and Transition

As teenagers, we go through many new journeys that shape us later on in life. These adventures are sometimes exciting or humorous, but they can also be frightening. You might be at home thinking that other people are going to judge you, or that you would rather handle the situation alone since you're the only one experiencing them.

The truth is, no matter what nationality or background you come from, we all share the same strains of society.

In the following pages; you will be presented with several different experiences teenagers have had with diverse changes or transitions in their lives. They wrote out their stories and what they learned from all that has happened to them.

These personal accounts are presented so that other teenagers around the world can see that they are not alone: dealing with moving to new environments, dealing with the consequences of your actions, death, and much more. This segment focuses on life altering events.

The stories were written by our generation so you could learn, or relate, and help you deal or cope with whatever it is you have going on in your life at the moment. Some parts will sound familiar while others will not, but when it all boils down to it, we are all teenagers living in the same world; going through the same crazy voyage of growing up.

18+

Prison Lived, Lesson Learned

There was a time in my life when it was out of control. It all happened when I started smoking weed and doing crimes to fund it. It was fun at first... but when I got caught I knew it was not fun at all but just plain old stupid...

I went to court—it lasted about 5 months till I was sentenced. The judge wasn't even lenient on me even though it was my first offence. They gave me a few chances: either go on the stand and grass on my co defendant or go to some crime prevention thing, but I didn't even go ahead with both those chances. I should have put more thought into it and went to that crime prevention thing 'cause it was the only chance I had to prevent me from going to prison...

In the end I got sentenced to 18 months, I don't know why but on the first night I broke down in tears...

I met someone who I knew and his wing was next to mine. He spoke to the 'screw' and the next thing I knew I was in his wing and sharing that room with him. He was a lot older than me, taught me a lot and was also a kind and caring person (even though he had a past about him). I stayed there with him for 'bout a month, they then moved me to another prison all the way in Dorset...

I stayed there throughout my sentence. I kind of made some business in there... for instance, if I give you a pack

(18+)

of crisps you gotta repay me 2 packs back next week, if you don't you're gonna have to give me 4 times the amount in the following week and that goes for anything— cigs, tobacco, pot noodles, etc. and if you don't repay it back you're gonna get it later in the shower and it's not the 'pick up the soap thing' you know!

While I was in there all I could think of was how long till my sentence ends...every day seemed like a year, it was dreadful... and the excitement and adrenalin kicked in when there was only a few days to go when I'm a free man again! I may have repaid it all back to society and may have come to terms with what I did, but the guilt still remains in me.

P.S: To all you youngsters or gangster wannabes who's reading this... going to prison is not a cool thing, you will miss valuable time in your life....

Anonymous

<u>Living Again</u>

Sometimes you think it will never happen to you, you see it on TV and you talk about it with your friends, you may even amuse yourself in hearing about it and even watch it. But you never think that it could happen to you.

I was walking home from my friend's house one night. It was the winter season and my body was freezing, I just wanted to get home as soon as I could.

I came across a crossroad where in order to get across, I would either have to wait for an opportunity to cross or take the underground which was much easier and quicker. Since I was cold, I felt I'd take the underground tunnel.

It was a long dark tunnel and you could see the light at the other end of the tunnel, I didn't think much of it but as I reached halfway through the tunnel, I heard a voice in the shadow:

"I never seen you here before."

I stood frozen in horror and shock, I couldn't speak.

"Na I ain't seen this boy before, what are your ends?"

I was too scared to speak, he was asking me where I lived, and I couldn't make out any clear words so I just pointed forward and uttered:

(18+)

"There"

"Na your chatting shit blud, what have you got for me?"

I knew what was going to happen; he was going to rob me. I remembered I had my phone, my house keys and my wallet on me.

I slowly summoned all my energy towards the other direction and as I was preparing myself to run, I felt a presence from behind me and before I could react, a hard solid object impacted with my eye.

The impact made me lose balance and I struggled to steady myself so that I wouldn't fall on the floor because if I fell on the floor, I knew it would be all over, I would be helpless.

With both of my arms shielding my injured eye, I gathered my senses and realized there was at least 3 of them; two were in front of me and the one who attacked me was behind me.

I tried to back away but one of them took grip of me and put me against the wall, I managed to shout help but it was so quiet that I assumed no one heard me. All of a sudden, one of them pulled out a sharp object and pulled it against my face. My body was in shock and my voice was paralyzed...

I finally got to the other end of that tunnel but I wasn't the same person as when I entered it. My body was beaten so much I could no longer feel anything, my mind was so frozen that I couldn't even think, everything I had was stolen and without even realizing it, I was home. I knocked on the door to find my little sister open it. I covered my bruised eye and walked into the house, avoiding everybody and heading into my room.

In my room, I left the light turned off, got into my bed and just laid there trying to figure out everything that just happened...eventually I fell asleep.

The next morning was when it hurt the most. My head was in pain, my arms and legs were aching and suddenly, without realising, tears began to fill my eyes... I was scared. My life would never be the same again. I would be too scared to go see my friends, scared to go out to the shops and scared to go school. Even the idea of opening my front door sounded terrifying.

You see, I used to be a very cheerful person before this and I never had a grudge against anyone. When my family asked me what happened to my eye, I said that I had a small accident on a funfair ride. They all bought it because they would never suspect that what happened that night would ever happen to me.

My life became very difficult, I would imagine that night over and over again in my head and what I would have done differently. Maybe if I had a weapon, it would have been different. My fear turned to anger, anger turned to revenge, revenge would turn back into fear of consequences, it would never end, I was helpless.

(18+)

My biggest fear was that I didn't know these people, it was dark at the time and I didn't know their faces. They knew me and I didn't know them, and because they attacked me near my house, they could have hung around my area which made me scared even more.

My worst nightmare came true when my mum asked me to go get some bread. I immediately built up a sweat and without thinking; I took a 5 inch knife from the kitchen and safely placed it in my pocket. Heading to the shop down the road I spotted a small hooded group outside the shop, I put one hand in my pocket where my knife was and I walked through them. I was expecting one to look at me; maybe he would recognize me and say something, maybe start trouble with me... I don't know what I would have done if he did...

They didn't pay any attention to me and I got into the shop safely, took a sigh of relief, bought the bread my mum asked for and ran home, past the gang. They were no longer a threat to me.

When I got home I felt so happy and free - I just overcame an obstacle to my fear and was starting to take on the world again... that's when my mum said the bread was expired so I had to go back to the shop to exchange it.

Upon reflection that night however I was still scared. Although going out to the shop made me feel better, the idea of either seeing friends outside or going school still scared me. But it got to the point where I had to go school again, I couldn't pretend being ill anymore and I had to overcome the obstacle like I had with the shop incident. Suddenly, images of all the things that could happen flushed into my mind:

What if I meet them on the bus?

What if they attack me again?

Who would help me?

I imagined all the scenarios which could have happened and I decided to arm myself again with a knife, but in my coat this time. I also had a metal pole in my school bag.

They made me feel comfortable and allowed me to go to school with ease. I wasn't worried about been caught because again, I'm not the type to be associated with these things so no one would suspect me.

I adjusted back into school life quite well. During school time my life was fine, however when it came to home time, my fears and alertness came up again.

The amazing thing was that nobody knew about this, not even my closest friends knew what I was going through, but they never suspected a thing.

I wanted to run away, to go to another city where my relatives stayed, but then I realized these things could happen anywhere and I shouldn't be trying to run away. What happened to me happened, I can't deny that, but I won't allow

(18+)

that to stop me from living my life, I won't allow the actions of these low lives to destroy my freedom and happiness.

I decided to stop carrying weapons with me now; I realized that I can't carry weapons forever. The truth was, I never intended to use them anyway, I just wanted to feel safe and protected. I also realized that I would probably end up hurting myself more than I would protect myself if an incident would ever occur.

Now, whenever I notice bullying or any form of violence in school, especially from the children below me, I strive to resolve them and prevent anyone from being hurt because to me, preventing violence and helping young kids to stray away from gang life and violence is my own way of healing my own emotional scars.

Anonymous

An Eye Opener...

I always thought that life is easy, I had everything as it was said— I was born with a silver spoon. I belonged to an elite rich family in Mumbai. As I was growing I was given everything. At the same time, it was made sure that I earned what I was given. For example if I wanted an iPod, I had to earn it by either proving myself with my grades or behaving in a deserving manner. That taught me to value things and be satisfied with what I have. Now that I have been so modest, let me be a little honest, I was at the same time a little spoilt, I never travelled in public transport, I had never walked to any place, I used to have the car at my disposal.

I had people working for me, to get my phone, shoes and pack my bag. I need not do anything. Now that I was used to such a lifestyle, I didn't know what was coming around. I had finally received my admission acceptance in the university and I was all set to go to London. I had no clue of what was heading my way. I reached my university with full excitement; with the help of my aunt I settled in very well.

I got all my supplies, I had my clothes nicely stacked into the cupboard, and I had set all my groceries in the kitchen — got enough to last me for a month. Now comes the fun part, what I had never realized was that my aunt was there the first time to do it for me, soon came the time when I ran out of my basic supplies of bread, butter, cheese etc. and now I had to go do my grocery shopping all by myself. At first I didn't know

(18+)

where to go, what to get, what are the brands that are good and that are bad. I spent 5 hours in the bloody grocery store and finally managed to get the bread, butter and cheese. Till today I keep on shifting the brands.

Then came the time of laundry, one has to run out of clothes sometime— that's the biggest lesson of all. Back home I used to get clean and washed clothes every single day— out here in London we have to do it on our own and so I went a whole month without washing. Finally the day came where if I didn't go laundry I would have to go naked to the university, so I asked a friend of mine to come with me. We entered the laundry room; it had 3 huge machines and 3 small. Luckily the day I went there was no one else there. The place had a weird smell, however ignoring that I removed all the dirty laundry and placed it in the big and attractive looking machine. To that my friend Sahan responded, "So in India do you dry your clothes before washing." With an embarrassed look I responded, "I put it in the dryer didn't I?" he laughed his head out.

He knew I had never done laundry before. Anyway moving on, I removed it and placed it in the washing machine "finally" and then tried to switch it on without any soap. So again Sahan told me what to do, now this is the worst what happened next: there were two machines one was for the soap and one was for the condoms, needless to say what must have happened next. I by mistake put the coins in the condom machine thinking the brands to be different soaps.

Finally I managed to get actual soap and I washed my clothes. We hence called that *The Mission Impossible*—my first ever laundry encounter.

The whole point about this was that the transition that took place from the person who had everyone to do things for him, I became a guy who knew how to do what seems like everything. Now, I can wash clothes, clean dishes and the biggest of all cook without burning down the kitchen! I had learnt a lot from this experience and have become more independent.

By Raheel Shah

18+

Wing it

A friend of mine once told me, 'Bar you might as well have been born a bird.'

With confusion I replied, 'what are you talking about?'

'It just seems to me like you wing everything.'

Until today I don't know if he was being serious or was just terrible at being funny, but it did make me realize something two years later during my last year of high school.

I learned in an American school system where before university you attended high school from 9th grade until 12th grade. 10th grade was coming to an end and I passed with sufficient grades to join the International Baccalaureate (IB). By this time I have become accustomed to choosing classes that require the least amount of work, which boiled down to in the IB from choosing between having a lot of hard work or a lot of even harder work.

It only seemed natural when I saw the choice for Theatre Arts that I would choose it. I figured it would be like drama that I have previously taken and wouldn't require too much attention from me—perfect class for winging. This was the best mistake I have ever made in my life.

My Theatre Arts teacher was probably the most liked throughout the school even though I wasn't too familiar with her yet. The first day of class she opened up her heart to us, so much that some even compared her to their own mothers. She was probably one the most interesting characters I have ever met. She was what seemed to me, unorganized but somehow knew where everything was. She would always be smiling except for when she would lose something urgent. Then she would walk around with a little frown looking under her organized mess of a desk, and when she would look up again regardless of whether she found it or not she would have a smile on her face. She made us keep a journal where we write about how we are feeling along with our emotions, ideas, learned things, and technical aspects that have to do with plays, stages, props, and everything to do with Theatre Arts. On our first day of journal entries she was proud of me for talking about the ensemble—the group of people that you work and perform with.

In the beginning our ensemble was weak and divided into groups. In the end we were all so close and could trust each other no matter what, something that would have been impossible if it wasn't for our teacher. My mind state at the point was that if I could write a bunch of mambo jumbo for this journal and do the least amount of work, I'll be able to pass; maybe with any other teacher but not with her.

The journal entries and projects that followed all got low marks and I couldn't understand why. The teacher finally sat me down and took my journal. She spent the next half an hour explaining to me the potential I had with creativity and theatre. She broke down my journals and performances and talked about my strengths and weaknesses. I don't know what it was but something in that conversation just clicked in my head and things made more sense. I understood my different views and perspectives when watching performances, things that interested me or that I would direct differently. With this she helped me build confidence in acting on a stage and taking a leading role, with many diverse characters. She helped me learn how to express my feelings about things through my writing more.

With all the help she gave me, my proudest moment was when I directed "Sure Thing" by David Ives. I took a relatively simple play to direct which made my teacher worry about the grade we get as directors. But I took what she taught and used my imagination, which got me lots of appraisal from the other teachers who deal with theatre.

I couldn't have done this without my two main actresses and my teacher. We started out in her eyes as a hopeless group of students, but we all grew closer to each other than any other group she taught. She would help us with our work, our hard work, but also let us have fun from time to time and bake us goods. We all knew her and her family closely. By the end of the year Theatre Arts did feel like a big family.

It was when I wrote my final 4000 word essay that I realized how much she's helped me develop. Not only was my grade higher in her class but in all my classes. I guess instead of helping me spread my wings and fly carelessly, she helped me shed my wings and walk passionately. She's a woman who made everybody she ever met a better person, and I know that I, just like all the others, will never forget her.

Alenka Dorrell you are in our hearts forever.

By Bar Segal

Choices... Do You Have the Guts to Dare?

Destiny is not a matter of chance, it is a matter of choice; it is not a thing to be waited for, it is a thing to be achieved.

Why do we have to make choices? This is what I thought when I had to choose something for myself. Something that would make or break my future as my whole life depended on what I decided then. I spent my whole birthday thinking about my studies. I was stuck. I didn't really know what to do in my life. I was just so clueless after I had finished my International Baccalaureate exams. All my friends had finished their examinations. Everyone knew what they wanted from their lives. They knew about their streams. A few got in the prestigious Indian Institute of Technology while the others got in their desired colleges because of their All Indian Engineering Entrance Exam scores. Some wanted to do Chartered Accountancy and so they gave their first set of exams for that while others, from IB, had begun their wholesome preparations. Some waited for their IB results so that they could go to either US or UK while some decided stay back in India and go to Indian colleges. I doubted if anyone was stuck like me.

I knew that I was in that situation because of what I had decided earlier when I had joined IB. I decided to let go Physics because I was very sure that I won't be doing Engineering or Medicine. I decided not to go to US and be here in my country because I love my country BUT the question was

WHAT NEXT? Whenever I met anyone, the first question they ask is *"What are you planning to do now that your IB is over?"* and I used to give them a blank look. Then I started saying the same thing that I used to tell everyone and believe me I was really tired of explaining the same ol' thing to all my friends and family.

My plan was to do something really extraordinary but the problem was I didn't know how. More than studying I wanted to do extra-curricular activities and social service topped that list of extracurricular work. I had already secured an admission in Symbiosis University at Pune but I was sure that I was going to cancel it once I got in either NM College or HR College because I wanted to be in Bombay. Then I wanted to prepare for my MBA entrance exam and Indian Civil Services exam. That was what my Dad had suggested and I COMPLETELY trusted him then. These were things that I had planned but how often do things go to our own plan? Man proposes—God disposes!

Today, my life has come a long way since I started my International Baccalaureate. Before the IB I was sure that I won't study Medicine. Engineering was still there in my mind. So I started to prepare for the IIT entrance exams. After I joined IB, I realized that engineering was not on the cards anymore and I thought of doing biochemistry. After a year in IB I understood that I liked Business more than sciences, so I conveniently chucked the idea of doing Biotechnology and/ or Biochemistry. After the IB I was left with many options and

18+

it was because of that range of options that I was confused. I hated the indecisiveness. Sometimes I thought that it would have been much better if I wouldn't have any option. At least I would have known WHAT TO DO IN LIFE!

How wrong was I! I am now in Hong Kong, merrily studying in an institution that respects me. I have a full scholarship, whole bunch of new friends, more knowledge about different cultures from the insights that I gain from my international friends and the best of all, more independence! This was possible only because I dared to make a choice to be different. I gave up my 'set' life in India and decided to go out of my comfort zone and take a risk, take a chance and lo! I have been blessed with an opportunity to shine!

I guess this is how life shapes up for an average teenager like me. at one point you don't know what is happening around and the very next moment you realize that it is the opportunity for you to go ahead and show the world who you are! All we need to do is take those chances!

By Gaargi Sharma

Ivan

Ivan was a big boy. His greasy coiled hair and his chubby face made him look like a baby, but no one would have ever dared to call him that, or call him any other names. Just Ivan. It was not his appearance that made him terrifying. For what I know from my previous school, his figure would have been the ideal victim for a bully. But here, no one dared to look at him for long. His eyes had a certain darkness that people try to avoid at all cost.

So what makes him terrifying?

He was intelligent. His words and insults were his best defensive and offensive weapons. His mysterious eyes gave the chill to shut anyone up. Sometimes, even the teachers seemed to fear him.

It was the first day of 6th grade when I first met Ivan. He was the biggest guy in the class, but sat in the front row. Being the last to class, I was "granted" the seat in the front row, next to Ivan, which no one seemed to like. He drew a line on our desk, dividing it in "half". He pointed at the smaller half, approximately a fourth of the desk, and said, "This is your half. Do not cross it." His words were simple, but so powerful and effective that it provoked a profound fear and uneasiness.

I was a new member of the school, but not a coward. I took out my eraser and rubbed the line off. Then, with a

18+

pencil, drew a line dividing the desk in the middle. I pointed at my half and said, "This is my half, but you can cross it." I smiled with a strained ease, and stared straight into his eyes. Eyes no one would dare to look into, eyes that swallowed every drop of confidence you had. My desire to avoid further harm was strong, but I forced myself to face his anger. Maybe this is the reason we became friends.

Ivan was not as bad as what people thought. He had hobbies and pastimes like everyone else. He liked music, and knew a lot more about computers than I did. Our little gang of two people slowly grew larger. We hurt no one, but were feared by everyone. We hung out at the mall, went to movies, played computer, and worn our time with jokes. From the terrorizing bully, Ivan evolved into a pleasant and generous friend, paying for our drinks, telling us jokes and standing up for us. He'd pay the extra tip when we finish at a restaurant, he'd plan trips out to amusement parks and he'd introduce us to girls. He was feared but admired at the same time.

However, there was one thing that all of us disliked about Ivan – his constant boasting. Ivan loved to praise his father and his wealth:

"My dad used to be a boxer, and could have gone pro...

"My dad plays billiards with the prime minister…

"My dad has bodyguards following him everywhere, because he's very important...

"My dad has a bulletproof car of which only 50 were made in the entire world…

"My dad…"

We bought his stories at first, but as we became older these stories were thought of as ridiculous lies and we all grew tired of hearing but never seeing his dad. In 8th grade, most of us grew taller than Ivan, but more importantly, we became more intelligent. He could not boss us around anymore, but was rather made fun of because of his size, which grew both vertically and horizontally, but did not change in proportion. His curses no longer hurt us and his punches weren't exactly powerful. Even the weakest one of us dared to joke about him because he would never be able to catch us.

I did not want to partake in insulting him, but his stories and the way he acted irritated me. We thought that by making fun of his boasts, he would feel that it was about time to stop.

"So when is your dad going to pick you up with that crazy Batman car of his?"

"He's on a business trip and shut up before I—"

"Ivan, you don't need to lie to be cool. I just

(18+)

wish you'd–"

"Mind you own business! You don't understand, and with you dumb friends you will never understand! Don't ever talk to me again!"

Ivan didn't care. He felt a sense of betrayal and began searching for new friends.

Ivan's new group of friends gave him what he wished for, but not friendship. They were impressed by his stories and followed his orders because they knew he could afford their expenses. Ivan liked it. He bought his friendship instead of working for it. Friendship that seemed to heal the deep wounds we've lashed on his self-esteem, but they were only painkillers, easing his pain temporarily.

His presence began fading and his grades glided down on a vertical slide. For a week, he did not show up to class and I began to worry. Despite his ridiculous stories, he was still a friend whom I did not wish to lose. I decided to make a visit.

Ivan never invited me over and it always bothered me. After a search and a call, I found his address and left in search for his house. It was on an aged street with bits and pieces missing from the pavement. The houses all looked the same: gray walls, brown fences, and a few trees to give them some colour. I stopped in front of Ivan's house. Looking at the broken fence and missing shingles, I wondered why his rich dad wouldn't pay for a nicer house. Through the windows, I saw his mother, her straight posture, perfect hair, tainted with a cheerless face and greying hair, all illuminated by a few flickering lights.

Ivan was not home. In the past week, Ivan returned late after dusk and left before sunrise. At first, his mother thought he attended after school activities, but later on, she saw him in the parks. He has been out with his new friends, drinking, smoking, doing graffiti, and ruining the city along with his life. His mother was worried to death, but couldn't do anything to help her stubborn teenager. I felt her anxiety, anxious of what her beloved son was becoming. Anxious of how and why that generous and pleasant friend would turn so miserable.

The door opened suddenly and Ivan appeared at the door, worn out and haggard. His gaze locked on to mine and I felt the ember set ablaze inside his eyes.

"What the hell are you doing here?" Ivan darted in the living room. He turned to his mom and screamed, "Mom! You can't just invite random people from school over!"

"But he's you friend. He was looking for you, so I told him to come in and wait for you."

"You don't care about my privacy! You don't care about me! Dad would never do things like this!"

18+

"Oh stop talking about dad. He is gone! You have to deal with me now!"

Ivan knocked over the dining table, falling to his knees and arms. Plates and glasses shattered at the landing on the ground. I felt his embarrassment and anger as he stumbled upstairs.

A sudden mixture of pity, anger, and guilt rushed through my mind. This is the reason he's been making those lies. This is why we've never seen his father, and all this time we just made a joke out of it. It was us, his friends, who had turned against him and betrayed him. We spent all this time destroying his charm and confidence, feeding his anger instead. It was not his new gang, but his best friends, who took what he had, and now it was our responsibility, my responsibility, to return it.

I stalled my way up to Ivan's room, a guilty kid who is about to confess and apologize for a stupid mistake, thinking of the best words to use to avoid the worst. Fear consumed my hope as pieces of glasses paved my way to his room. After a long silence and three knocks on his door, I took the courage to enter his room.

As the darkness in the room filled up with the glimmering light of the hall, the most terrifying shock of my life shattered my thoughts. I roared from the bottom of my lungs, with pain, anger, and horror, but the terror swallowed the sound. The guilt still haunts my dreams at night. That image of the final struggles of an aching soul, destroyed under the pressure of the 'perfect' people of society will forever wrench at the remaining strings of my sanity.

By Zifeng Wei

Home Away!

I was extremely excited about finally leaving to Canada for further studies. I would be pursuing my Bachelors degree from abroad just as I always wanted. I was excited about living alone without any restriction, I could do what I want and I didn't have to report to anyone. Finally freedom, I was anxious to get out of here and be independent and not be dependent on people to do my work.

Finally that day had arrived I was packed and all ready to go, my parents and friends escorted me to the airport. They were going on about how they would miss me and what I should do there in cold and how I should call my parents every day. As they blabbered on my mind had already wandered off to Canada; I could feel the snow in my hand, the cold breeze gushing through my hair. I could see myself playing snowballs and wearing whatever I wanted to. At that point my dad told me we had reached the airport. The whole ride I dreamt, and that's all I had been doing for the past 2 months.

Those twenty hours of flight journey seemed like ages to me, I could not wait for the pilot to announce to fasten our seatbelts in order to land. I had finally landed in the land of freedom, people seemed so nice and courteous and helpful. The immigration lady wished me luck in my future endeavors in life. It all seemed nice and amazing at first.

I finally got to my room that I was sharing; my partner was from east London and an amazing guy who taught me a lot of new football tricks. We had instantly clicked and had become good friends. Everything was going smoothly for the first month. I had started to get to know everyone and get the hang of how the university works. Plus I had met all my professors and started building my repo with them.

After a month I started missing home and this was when my partner left for his internship for two months. I was all alone in the room thinking and I realized I had never missed home like this before. I just wanted to mom and dad and to take the next flight out to see them. I was missing my friends and all the late night drives that we used to have. I was missing the food that used to be served outside on the roads in the most inhumane places. I was missing everything.

I started to realize that this was not me, I enjoyed the freedom for a month but now I was not happy anymore. I was missing my mom scolding me if I did something wrong, I was missing those small details that used to take place at home and make me feel that I am a part of the family and I belong here.

I had realized that I had not settled down yet and I was just fascinated with all the change. But as I got settled the fascination was over. I realized what I really wanted; I wanted to be home, with my family. I had lost it completely and so I ended up calling my dad, first thing I told him was how much

18+

I love him and the rest of the family. I told him I had to come home and that this place was not for me. I told him I could not live here I had to come home.

Somehow he knew this was coming, so what he did first was to tell me to calm down and that he would be happy with whatever I decide provided that this time I think it through. He told me everyone would have settlement issues in the beginning, it was up to us on how we deal with it. He said that I should give it a try and not eliminate it completely. It took me three months to settle down, and become comfortable with my life again.

Today I am happy that I am studying here but at the same time eager to finish and finally get back home. I call home almost every second day and I talk to my friends almost every day on Internet. I go home every holiday and make sure I work hard for the course and make my parents proud. I'm sure a lot of you can relate when it comes to moving to a new place and living by yourself. Give it some time to get used to, and if it doesn't feel right after a while, it probably means you should try something else. Luckily I waited long enough to realize it isn't that bad.

Anonymous

Different Places, Different Faces

Well where to start. My name is Eric Janse, I'm 19 years old and I come from Holland. I have two brothers and two sisters. My experience is about moving to Hungary and eventually moving back to Holland after living in Hungary for 6 years.

We moved to Hungary when I was six. At the time I was really excited going to a country that I had never even heard of before. We were told a couple of weeks before that that we were moving there. The reason actually was that my dad worked in the Czech Republic at the time and we were moving so he could be closer to home and later he'd work for the same company in Hungary.

My parents already decided what school we were going to, the A.I.S.B. At first, the classes were full so I had to wait a month before I could actually go to school. In the mean time I stayed home and went to lots of places with my mom and dad. I didn't mind it at all, I loved going everywhere and Hungary is a beautiful country.

A month later the school called saying they could place me in a class. At first I didn't like the idea at all going to school in a strange country because I could only speak Dutch and a few words in English, so I didn't really know what to expect.

So I went to school and after a few weeks I started to adapt and it became pretty normal speaking English. I didn't know

18+

all the words yet but that didn't matter at all because during school time I went to E.S.L (English as a Second Language) and there the teacher helped children with their English. I believe I had 2 years of E.S.L and after that I didn't need it anymore.

It wasn't hard to make friends either. The kids were all very friendly and so were the teachers. In those six years I went from Kindergarten to 1st grade, 2nd grade, 3rd grade, 4th grade and to 5th grade. In the mean time the school had moved to a new location and it was great! I think it's the nicest school I've ever seen but at the end of 5th grade we heard that we were going back to Holland.

I think if there is anything I regret it is me having to go away from a country I had become to see as my home and just leaving it behind with all my friends. I had loved living there, just like I said before it's a beautiful country and I have a lot of memories of that place.

In the end it turned out pretty well because despite having to go away, leaving it all behind me, it turned out that if I finished school there I would still have to go back to Holland to start a new study. I would have to go away from my parents and my brothers and sisters.

If I look at me now, I'm learning to be an Aircraft Maintenance Technician! The study is great; its hard work but I don't really care, the most important thing is that I started a new life in Holland and have new friends and I'm learning to be something that I really like.

I think that what I'm trying to say with this story is that there are some things that are really great in life and sometimes they go away but there will always be a new great experience waiting for you and no matter what, it will get better. This is not meant to sound tragic but it's the truth. For instance I hated going away from Hungary, the great experiences, and my friends but it all turned out great for me. And guess what? If there is one great thing that I ever experienced as a kid it is going there. I learned to speak English almost perfectly and in this study it's going to be the language I'm gonna have to be good in because all the maintenance data is in English and most foreign technicians all speak it.

Well, this was pretty much my story, I hope it may help some of you guys out there to know that everybody experiences things that maybe they don't like at first but it will always get better.

By Eric Janse

18+

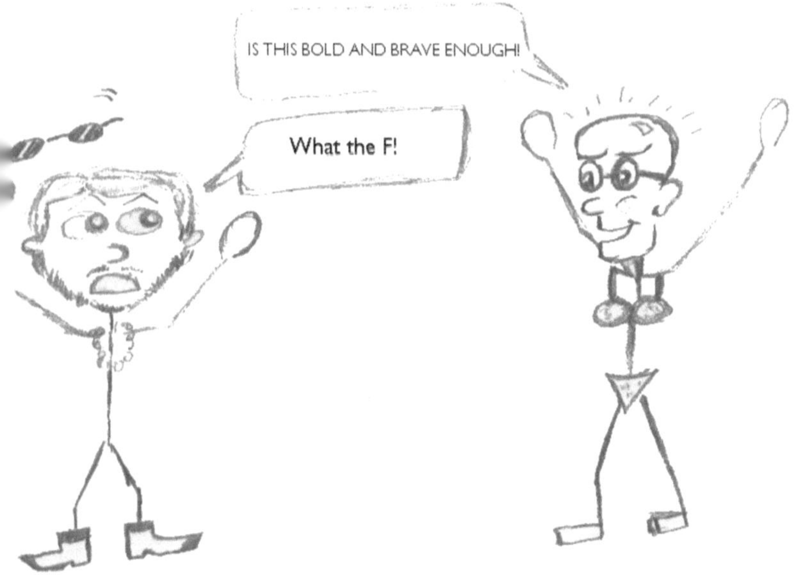

Love and Relationship

In life we come across many phases that make us a different person all together. Some of those times are when we find are loved ones. There are some relationships that seem to be the best thing that has ever happened; some are just bad mistakes that leave people with scars for life. Further in this chapter you will read stories from different experiences, good and bad with their fellow loved ones. These stories not only talk about how they broke up or how they asked their partners out, but it also talks about how these events have affected them in their life and people around them.

When you enter a relationship, it's not just you that are in it, but your friends, family and close loved ones are the external factors that affect it. One decision of yours could lay an impact on the rest as well. I learnt from reading these stories how relationship and love is not just words, but has deeper meaning to it than that. Love and relationship are vital tools used in carving one's life.

18+

Theo and Theresa

He was talking about her again. It annoyed me a little bit although it shouldn't. Yeah, he was her boyfriend for the last 3 years and my friend for 10 months but there was something about him that arrested my attention...something about him that made me listen to his every word for any length of time. His name was Theo and he was everything to me—all that I wanted, but obviously he didn't know that. More than a crush? I think so.

Thought to myself, if I could talk to him enough, be his friend and confidante he would want to spend as much time with me as what I craved with him. So emails, phone calls, meeting up to watch the football game at his house and the occasional games nights with his cousins became the norm. We had loads of fun together but we were only friends and it was frustrating because we became closer and closer. You have no idea how close I came to revealing it all to him. Sometimes I would stare at him and shout in my head:

Why is it so hard for you to see that I like you? Are you that blind!

Theo's girlfriend's name was Theresa. Awww, how cute... their names even matched up. It made me sick—or maybe just sickly jealous.

(18+)

Theresa lived in Uxbridge—it seemed a million miles away from where we lived in Edmonton, although it was basically London, or just on the outskirts. I hadn't even seen pictures of her—I tried to avoid them at all costs. I'd say:

"Nah Theo, I would rather see her in person first than look at pictures—that's a bit odd don't you think?"

Obviously he'd think that my view was weird but I would laugh it off and change the topic with seamless swiftness.

And so the glorious day finally came when Theo exclaimed:

"Theri's coming down for the weekend to come see me"

I was thinking—

> *Here we go again, yet another weekend where I'm not going to see you and I have to think about how you're cuddling up in the arms of your beloved Theri...*

What wouldn't I do to trade places with her? Hardly nothing I guess.

Saturday came quickly... I think because I was worrying so much about meeting Theo's girlfriend. Would she be able to tell that I liked her boyfriend by just looking at me? Would she give me the cold shoulder all day? Well I kind of hoped she would because that would make my life a lot easier—I wouldn't like her and wouldn't give a damn if I got up to stuff with her man. I liked that idea so I kept that image... Theresa the bitch... I hoped she'd live up to it.

I was standing at the train station waiting for Theo to arrive—he was bringing Theresa with him. He had picked her up from her aunt's house which wasn't too far away but she was unfamiliar with the area. Her aunt had apparently just moved into a new house and it was her first time staying there. So there I was... waiting...patiently waiting. Okay okay okay, I was not patiently waiting—I was biting my finger nails and pacing like a maniac.

I stopped.

I saw two figures coming around the corner at the train station—it was Theo and Theresa... holding hands and talking frantically to one another. She was beautiful and quirky—wore skinny jeans and funky trainers. She tied her hair back in a messy ponytail that screamed function over fashion—she seemed cool. She came up to me and said:

> "Hailey, hi! We finally meet—I hope I didn't keep you waiting too long..."

> She gave me a hug.

> "The stupid trains are so unreliable on the weekends—it's absolutely ridiculous."

> "I know right—I've got the same issue

18+

visiting my grandparents on the weekends. Don't worry about it."

I looked at Theo,

"You okay Theo? You look tired man."

I gave him a hug.

We went to have pizza and chilled out together for the rest of the day—it was fun and I didn't feel like a third wheel in the slightest.

Five months passed and Theresa and I became close—not as close as Theo and I... she never spoke about their issues with me—she had her best friends for that. What amazed me most about their relationship was how comfortable they were with each other keeping friends of the opposite sex. They were really mature and I admired that.

One day Theresa invited me over to hang out. We saw each other like twice a month, most times with Theo but this time he was away on some paintballing trip with his guy friends.

So I went over and she was her regular bubbly self. We sat down and chatted about random stuff before settling down to a chic flick and popcorn. Theresa got up and brought some alcohol in the room—a bottle of wine and a couple beers. She drank over half of the wine and was a little tipsy. This is when she started chatting—I mean chatting a lot.

Theresa started talking about Theo and how their relationship seemed rosy but she wasn't really happy. She said it was like they only connected as friends and as much as she tried it couldn't get deeper. She hated the fact that he loved her and she couldn't feel the same way about him.

I have to admit I was a little bit confused. I mean this girl had the best guy in the world—she had what I wanted and was not appreciating it at all. Anyway I listened—I could see she needed to let it all out and I wanted to hear where the problem was anyway. Despite my curiosity and my open mindedness, nothing could have prepared me for what Theresa was about to say and do next.

She started to whisper and I knew the alcohol was taking its toll on her.

"I can't hear you Theri—speak up,"

All I could hear was her mumbling so I went closer to her—

"Theresa, say that one more time."

She suddenly pushed my shoulders into the sofa, looking at me in an awkwardly intimate way and said:

"I like you Hailey... I really like you."

Before I could say anything she kissed me

18+

and in shock, confusion and anger I pounced up and shouted:

"What are you doing man? That is nasty! You have a boyfriend and I'm... I'm his friend okay! This is not right Theresa, I'm gonna go."

I just did not know what to think. I felt betrayed and dirty although it really was not my fault.

Theresa and Theo finally broke up although it took months after the incident that occurred between me and her. I didn't end up telling Theo till quite a few months after they broke up. The good thing was that Theo and I are still friends. I'm still freaked out by his ex (I love saying that) so I don't really speak to her—only when I have to. Now the great thing is that I confessed to Theo that I liked him and we decided to take it really slow and see what happens. I'm cool with that and I much rather build something substantial than something that is just based on comfort like what he and Theresa had. I cannot imagine being with someone for three years and not loving them. Doing that is such a waste of time and someone always gets hurt—I never want to end up like that.

Anonymous

It Happens to Boys

There was a girl that I had liked for a long time. Her name was Natalie. I met her through another friend of mine and we hit it off really well. During that time, we flirted a lot with each other and we trusted each other when it came to secrets. I thought I'd finally take the chance and ask her out as my chances were very high. I even had a small speech prepared.

So that day when we went out and strolled by the riverside, I confessed to her,

> "I know we've known each other for a long time, and I think we become close together, much more than friends. I really like you Natalie so maybe we should go out together, it'd be really fun."

There was that awkward silence where she was probably taking in everything I just said, and then she answered:

"I'm sorry Tung, I just don't think I'm ready for a relationship at the moment. I do like you too but I don't want a boyfriend."

I felt a slight ache in my heart, but I was cool enough to manage it.

It's ok Natalie, as long as were still friends and all."

(18+)

I didn't mean what I said but you got to act fine, don't wanna break down and cry.

"Yea we're still friends Tung," she smiled and playfully hit my arm.

That night we ended the night with a hug; a very short one at that.

Ever since then, I haven't spoken to her as much as I used to, you get the odd, "Hi how are you doing?" but nothing deep or interesting.

Then some time later on, I get a message on my MSN, it's from Natalie!

The first thing she said was boring, like,

"Hi, what have you been up to?"

And then she says:

"Can I ask you something Tung?"

"Yea sure, what is it?"

"...would you like to go out with me?"

"What?!" I couldn't believe it!

She continued:

"I been thinking about it a lot and I think I do like it...so why not? :-)"

My heart pounded. I typed back:

"Well yea I guess we could still go out...Sure ok" (cool emoticons)

She typed back:

"O I'm so happy Tung! (Kisses)"

"So I guess we should meet up sometime then huh?" I asked.

"Yea sure sweetheart, I give you my number now because I have to go, call me tomorrow ok?"

"Ok Natalie, take care."

After she was gone, I was so over the moon.

The next few weeks were fun. All my friends knew about her and were happy for me, my Facebook and Bebo status all said *In a Relationship,* and had lots of positive comments from all my friends.

The phone calls with her were good, boring but nice. All we talked about was what we did that day and what we were doing now. I decided to arrange a meeting finally. It was to be at the riverside tomorrow at 1pm.

(18+)

We met each other at the train station; she greeted me with a fazed smile which was odd to me. We hugged and then held hands, talking as we walked to the riverside.

The conversation was mostly about her friend, the good and the bad things about her. I always found gossip to be good for conversation.

We sat down at a bench and I told her to lean onto me.

She did and at that moment, I felt so content and happy.

Then she spoke,

"Tung, I have to tell you the truth."

Destroyed the moment!

"Yea sure, what is it Natalie?"

"...I don't think it's working out"

Silence...

"Why, what happened?"

> "The truth is Tung, I've been depressed lately. I had an argument with my friend, I was telling her how I didn't like her new boyfriend and she attacked me back, saying that I could never get a boyfriend and that I was too ugly."

I understood what that meant.

"So in other words, you're just using me to make yourself feel better."

"I'm so sorry Tung."

"I guess its ok Natalie, its fine."

I lied, it wasn't fine. I was hurt and betrayed, my emotions were played and now that she was feeling better, she probably thought she could throw me away.

I tried to make things positive, generate a few laughs throughout the whole date, but in the end, I was just glad it was over. I didn't express to her how I felt about what happened. The embarrassing part was telling everybody else what happened; all my friends on Facebook, Bebo, everywhere...

I decided to just leave it and give it some time to see if people would forget. It was just amazing to see how her self-esteem was so bad that she would go to such extremes to feel better. Maybe in life, we should really learn to love ourselves first before loving others, otherwise someone is going to get hurt and it would usually be ourselves...

By Tung Nguyen

(18+)

Feelings of Lust

I had been out with Hadley a couple of times but I never quite opened up to him about anything. I never disclosed my private thoughts or feelings and let him do most of the talking. Then one day we went out for dinner and I started to like him a little bit more than I was willing to admit. I lay in bed night after night tormented with dreams of lustful desire for him. Hadley's beautiful soft hands roaming all over my body, my soft moans of pleasure. Our first kiss, his lips biting mine as his hands coaxed my hair. I woke up night after night feeling a little ashamed and wondering what I should do about my new found feelings. Day after day after talking to Hadley on the phone he left me reeling with confusion, did he like me in that way or did he just like me as a friend? Too scared to ask him about his feelings for me I decided to leave it as something for him to figure out on his own.

I carried on with miserable feelings of lust to someone that wanted nothing more than friendship. The next time I met up with Hadley I forced myself to act like I didn't care when deep down I was struggling with myself. Talking to me about his personal experiences he suddenly realised that I was being very quiet.

"You need to let yourself go; you act like you're nervous," he said.

"Is there something more that you want from me?" He asked

"...because if there is you should tell me."

I insisted that I had a lot on my mind and I was happy with the way things were.

In the weeks that followed I stopped myself from calling him in the hope that my growing feelings would fade but it just made things worse. Night after night dreams of his hands caressing my body and my moans of pleasure continued to dominate my mind.

After almost a month of not talking to Hadley I decided to call and catch up with the latest developments in his life. I called several times and to my avail he didn't pick up. Realising that he had probably forgotten about me I fell into a deep dark hole of self loathing and depression. I cried myself to sleep at night. Then after a few days of self loathing, I went to the nearest club and grabbed a random guy. The night was filled with lustful noises and at one point the neighbours had to knock on the door to ask if everything was okay. He was soft and gentle but yet very aggressive in his lovemaking and I couldn't contain my moans. He made me feel like a woman; and like something which I had been longing for had finally become attainable but alas this feeling was just for the moment.

(18+)

The next morning I woke up in another man's bed with feelings of shame.   I left as quickly as I could. Waiting at the bus stop I felt like everyone was watching me. At one point I decided to look at the floor so that I wouldn't have to look anyone in the eye.

Now months later as I walk through the streets I look at a man and wonder if he was the one that I shared a bed with, not having his number is one thing but not even remembering the way he looks is another. I am so lucky that I didn't catch any sexual diseases and vowed to myself that the next man I would give my body to would be someone that meant more to me than just a one night stand.

Anonymous

Love = war

I had heard and seen in movies that high school is a sea where love is war and politics is life. I never used to believe that and I always told myself if it is, then I sure as hell won't get involved. But we all know life's a bitch and fate's the ugly sister. I started my high school in Sweden where I used to live and had gone to boarding for 5 years. I developed a little social problem where I would judge people early on, but it really helped when it came to finding loyal friends.

My high school had a reputation of students who belonged to filthy rich families; needless to say they were all snobby douche bags. Although I belonged to an elite rich family I was never seen to be a snob, and a douche bag of course. During the beginning era of my high school life I would stay quiet mostly observing my fellow colleagues. It always intrigued me how the my schoolmates either embraced the fact that they were rich and try to show off every penny or rebelled and pretended like they didn't have any.

I have done many things during my school life that I am not proud of particularly with individuals. These incidents often take place when you have a very close friend. Knowing how things used to take place in our school between guys and girls I had decided to stay away from relationships. Trust me, breaking up with a girl is one thing, but breaking up with a girl who owns a credit card with no limit, that my friend, will

(18+)

cost you the wind shield of your car, and a helicopter to get it off school's roof (figuratively speaking of course).

I had seen enough to understand that getting into one is not the right thing to do right now with all the work given out and being new in school. I had firsthand knowledge that it would just be a distraction; therefore I decided to keep away from these relationships.

It was only when I finally got into a rhythm with my school work and new found friends with no relationships to worry about that life decided to screw with me. You probably wonder how I found friends in the school when it seems like all I do is negatively judge. Well, I guess when you break down their façade of bullshit, you learn the parents are often to blame, giving more green than red. This makes them more humane and more bearable. It was my best friend that had to pay for the life style that I have chosen.

My best friend's girlfriend and I became partners for biology since she was in my class and we knew each other from my friend. Group meetings, study sessions, and general get together for homework assignment, makes a lot of time spent together. I could go into details of eventually we got the highest grade on a project and decided to celebrate over champagne… well the truth is I did. The makers of this book asked me to take it out. It was really detailed, and she was blonde, also a D-Cup. Imagine what you guys missed out on, blame those guys not me!

I often get irony wrong but I'm sure you could find some here. The fact that I opted for a life style that focuses on work and ignores the sexual tensions of a teenager led me directly where I hoped not to go. Or maybe that I thought my schoolmates were douche bags and when I finally get a close friend, I turn out to be the biggest asshole. The point is when you deprive yourself in life with the hope of a better future; you'll often find that you look back and wish that you did things differently.

By Anonymous

(18+)

Their Point of View

I used to work in a pizza parlour whilst I was in college. I thought I should get a job while I was studying to get some extra spending money.

I only worked there for a month and I already had a manager who was a complete trashcan!

His name was Jim and whenever I saw him, he would never joke around or smile. In fact, he was very serious all the time.

One time when I saw him come in, I asked how he was doing, his response was, "have you washed the dishes yet?"

On another occasion, our new recruit Alice kept messing up on the till because she didn't understand the button. Jim stepped in and shouted at her right in front of the customers. The girl was probably around my age and she burst into tears. Jim didn't console her or anything, he just carried on with the till and gave the customer their change while she stood there crying in front of him.

I brought her into the staff room to cheer her up, she was still in shock and shaken. Jim came in a few minutes later and instead of apologising said, " We need someone at the till Alice, could you do that?"

That really annoyed me and I couldn't understand his rudeness and why he was so unsympathetic.

At the end of my shift, I risked my job by challenging him. I was so angry that it eventually had to come out. I told him how he was so horrible to Alice and even to send her back to work without an apology, how he doesn't treat any of the workers right and how he's not a good manager for not training Alice properly to make sure she understood the till.

He attacked back,

"What do you know!? You don't know me! I tell you what to do and you do it. And that's it. Don't give me that nonsense about caring and apologising! She knows why she's here; she wants money just like you do. If you want the money, you better do as I say too!"

A week later, he got fired from his job. Higher management heard about what happened and thought it was unacceptable so he had to explain himself in the main branch.

The new manager who replaced him at our branch was actually in the meeting when Jim was fired.

Apparently, around the time I worked there, Jim's wife passed away due to cancer and because they both worked and shared financial issues together, he couldn't manage the bills on his own so he lost his house and most of his possessions.

(18+)

He also had to pay a lot of money to the funeral director to give her a good burial.

As a result, he was financially broke and emotionally distressed. He was finding it difficult to manage the job and he didn't appear to have any family members around. So he was all alone...

It actually hurt me when I heard that. I was releasing all my anger against him but he was right, I didn't understand him at all. I took a moment to reflect on what happened. Alice seems to have forgiven him but I was hurt because I was the one who attacked him. Sure, what he did was wrong but if I had actually understood why he was like that, maybe I wouldn't have been as aggressive against him as I was, whether he did deserve it or not. I would have been more forgiving.

I only saw things from my point of view. I never considered his point of view and what he was going through.

The manager actually told me that before I worked here, he heard that Jim was actually very friendly and smiled and joked a lot.

I never saw him again since he got fired, but I really hope his is doing well with his life now and that he would forgive me for what happened back then.

By Thomas

Waiting and Then Moving On...

It's often said that during the years of schooling one is bound to develop a liking for a particular person from the opposite sex. Now this sounds very bookish and nerdy so let me say it in simple terms. When we are young we develop crushes for the opposite sex. This happened during my school days back in a town called Pune in India. My friends often said that I liked this one girl who had recently joined school. They would tease anyone who they thought were either becoming good friends, or just do it for the heck of it.

Now at that point, I had no feelings for the girl, but we had become good friends and she was part of our group. With the continuous teasing one does tend to tilt towards a possibility to like the person. At least that's what I experienced. One night after the Christmas party one of my very close friends came up to me and asked me,

"Do you like her?"

And I said no looking straight into his eyes. To that the only thing he said was,

"Either you are a good liar or you don't like her."

At that point I gave it no thought and just laughed through it. During the weekend I thought over the events that had taken place and then thought over what my friend had said.

(18+)

I was always there to help them and was always going to, but with her was it just friendship or was it more? For the first time I woke my friend up and told him that he might be right. At first he could not react since he didn't understand and then later on he started laughing and didn't stop. Seriously when someone is talking about his crush the other person should not laugh. However he told me to give her a call the next day and just start to talk to her and spend some more time with her. I didn't see how that would have helped but there was no harm in trying.

So I gave her a call and started talking about some stupid computer software that I knew inside out; there had to be some conversation starter. As she went on explaining I could not resist and I asked her out. She was in shock for a minute and then she gave the answer that I never wanted to hear,

"You are an amazing person, but I don't see you that way."

Long after that, our friendship grew and we spent more time together. We were still friends but my feelings had increased over time. This I realized on the last day of school when we all were going to get separated. She left for abroad, she was not going to be around us anymore and I had to, for the last time, tell her again, so I did. Her response to that was,

"What's the point of saying this now?"

Time passed by, soon it had been 4 years since that incident and I still liked her. This time, my friends told me that it was time to move on. I agreed to that, it had been 4 years. It was four long years of waste. I was waiting for her and I didn't let anything else happen in my 4-year high school life. That was it, I had to take control of my life and move on. It was not worth it.

So the long lasting wait of 4-years was over and I finally decided to move on with my life. To be honest it, has always been a one-way thing so it was nothing to do with her. Frankly I was ok since I selected to be that way. You don't always get what you want.

By Dheer Shah

(18+)

Emotions- Where Did They Disappear?

It was Friendship Day a week ago and throughout the whole day texts were flooding in. Everyone was wishing, "*Happy Friendship Day,*" even to those who are hardly in touch or cannot be considered as friends. Same happens on Valentine's Day. People just send greeting cards or texts or even gifts to each other with no specific reason. It appears more of a fashionable activity than emotions.

Have you ever wondered that our life has been reduced to a keyboard? Be it computer, laptop, cell phones or television? Keys and keys alone hold the key. We are so busy with our daily routine that we remember friends/relatives only on Friendship Day or birthdays and when we do, an SMS or a forwarded mail does the job! How convenient? Isn't it?

When we have time we are hooked to these keys: games, photos, instant messaging. What the heck! In the middle of a hectic schedule I remember an old friend and scores of things I wanted to say. But it takes courage to make a call, work is the first and last thing on mind so it's easy to type an SMS and push "OK". I wonder if there are really emotions left, I doubt it myself.

However, life has become comparatively easier and less burdened without emotions. Chatting is outdated, Facebook is the new passion! I make as many as friends as I can. Wall post the people whom I don't know—they don't care for me, but I think I have friends. No emotions needed! If I don't like the person I can just ignore him. If I don't feel OK, just log off! No more interest: delete mails or just don't reply. No emotional burden. It's easy, no arguments, no heart breaks, no pains.

Life has become smooth as there's no sense of loss and nothing to claim. Gone are those days when fear of losing loved ones kept relationships alive! Log off from one site and you can find more friends on some other; it's quite easy to make new/true friends! It's quite easy to flirt! The dangerous thing is that we are not feeling the vacuum. Everything's becoming electronic! Technology has made life painless. What is the difference between machines and human beings? Obvious answer was machines don't have emotions. Now? I wonder...

By Gaargi Sharma

(18+)

Heart Break...

Every girl falls in love…and most girls experience having their heart broken. I moved to a new country with a very different culture to my own and felt very insecure, intimidated and somewhat alone until I met the special person I fell in love with. He helped me settle in, helped me adapt to my new surroundings, made me feel comfortable and safe and happy in a place I never thought I would be. He was someone I relied on, someone I would share everything with and someone I cared for more than anything. I felt so in love, so happy and so comfortable that when it ended, it felt as though it was the end of the world.

He managed to move on and moved countries, yet I was left with all the memories and went back to feeling insecure and alone. At the time I was lucky enough to have good girlfriends that helped and supported me when I was upset, but the hurt and pain never seemed to go away. I had never had my heart broken before; therefore I was lost and didn't know exactly how to cope. It took a while for the tears to stop and I gradually started to move on with my life. I knew I had to stop reminding myself of all the good times and start learning to be independent again.

Although it was hard, I realize now that I should have been telling myself- he left you for another girl, he doesn't care anymore, he isn't the person he used to be and he isn't the only one out there for you. Instead I chose to believe that maybe somehow he would change, or would want to sort things out.

There is no easy way of dealing with a broken heart but my advice is, think of the relationship as a great memory that you will never forget and something you should smile about when you look back on it. Realize sooner rather than later that if it's meant to be, it's meant to be. If not try to move on, remember who you were before you met that person and open yourself up to other people. You never know, you might just fall in love again. I found that once I had started to pull myself together I went out and got a new haircut, had a nice night out with the girls, and began to feel single and sexy again! With everything bad, comes something good. I promise that no matter how you feel at the time, it can only get better.

Anonymous

(18+)

He Deserves to Come First

I am Christian. I love Christ and I enjoy worshipping and having fellowship as a group because you feel the love—you feel the presence of complete devotion and submission of all your problems to God. You know he can handle it, you know He loves you, you want to love Him and life is great... life is bliss.

Yes! University was starting. New friends, a new environment, new responsibilities and new experiences—it was like getting ready to go on holiday. Before I started University I had a boyfriend—we had love, we dated for a long time and we knew each other inside out. Yeah, we had our problems just like every couple but we worked on them all—I was happy.

As time slipped through my hands I subconsciously dropped a couple things in my life... some important things. I slowly but surely went out with my family less, speaking to my friends became a thing of the past and going to church... well, only when my boyfriend was going to be there. So you can see where this is going—if my boyfriend wasn't doing it, I wouldn't do it. But don't confuse this for me dropping things purposefully, I didn't realise I was doing this.

Not long after my boyfriend and I went our separate ways our relationship broke down and I was devastated. I cried for a long time and found it hard to deal with the loss of him...

the loss of us. What was I supposed to do? He said to do new things and it would get easier but it was far easier said than done. I just did not know what to do with myself.

Who am I? Do I really deserve this? How can someone you love so much just get rid of you like that? The tears would follow and I would feel low, angry and pathetic.

I decided to email a Christian advisor I didn't know. She encouraged me to read my Bible and talk to God about everything—my feelings, my betrayals, moving on and finding myself again. It was hard. I felt like God would not want to hear me because I had forgotten Him. I had also forgotten my family and friends.

That night I collapsed onto my knees and cried for the last time. I cried because I longed for true love and understanding. I cried because I wanted a healthy balance in my life and I wanted someone to love me with all my imperfections. The tears burnt my face that night—my face stripped from being so dry and I was dehydrated... but I felt good. I was happy. I was relieved. I felt like all my burdens were dropped and submitted to God. That night was the beginning of learning to balance what is important in life, the beginning to knowing me and the beginning to truly understanding why I am Christian and why I and so many other people put God first.

Anonymous

(18+)

Dorian

A girl falls in love with guy, guy uses her. We all know someone who's been in that situation before. It never ends well and the person in love always ends up feeling pitiful and miserable. A friend I knew not so long ago, we'll call him Dorian, went through what most people go through in life, rejection. He wore his heart on his sleeve and fell in love too quickly, always getting hurt. Dorian would tell a girl he liked her and get rejected too often. After more than a year of this Dorian's heart simply dug its way back into a dark hole and covered itself with meaningless one night stands. His emotions still ran deep but his courage to show his true feelings just seemed to disappear. Humour and charm would get him the morphine of sex and cover up his real wants.

There was a party one day when a girl he humoured and charmed for several weeks asked him to be her significant other. Without considering the girl's emotions and having just sex on his mind he agreed swiftly. The girl was so in love with Dorian that she did not realize how he did not love her like she loved him. "I love you" she would declare, "Aw thanks baby that's sweet" would be his reply. Dorian only met her when his friends were around, that way he wouldn't really have to talk to her. It seemed like the only time they spoke would be when they were intimate, if only just a few shared words. After several months of dating, Dorian grew bored and tired of having to cover up his tracks of infidelity and simply just sent her a text saying, "We're breaking up", as young teenagers all trying to impress one another we high fived him and joked about, "Now that is how you treat a woman!" Just boys being boys after all.

It's always sad to think that 15 taps of the finger could shatter a heart. The girl would constantly wonder why, if it's something she did and promising that she would change. Dorian being Dorian and using every method to ignore her and giving her evasive answers was able to continue with his life. A week passed and the girl still did not give up. A third week passed followed by a month and still she could not understand what it was. Crying helped a little, talking to her friends helped more, but nothing could help her move on without an answer for what would make him suddenly stop loving her.

Eventually a year would pass and Dorian would forget about the girl, and the girl pretended to move on. It was at a party when they would meet again later. The girl's heart would beat fast and old feelings surfaced. Dorian with a big intoxicated smile grabbed his crotch. They left home together that night, only for the girl to be thrown out the next morning. Feeling more crushed than she had ever felt before, her sadness turned into anger. She spent the following weeks trying to make him jealous. Meeting with his friends, going to parties with them, and making sure he witnessed all of it. Dorian, emotionally retarded, just felt happy for his friends.

(18+)

It was the day he had a house party that changed everything. The girl would hook up with his friend while he hooked up with another girl. Dorian and his new female friend were in his room. Out of anger, spite, and jealousy, the girl took Dorian's friend into his room. She pulled her new friend and just took him into the bed right next to Dorian. Not understanding what was happening Dorian's new female friend quickly left the room. Dorian out of anger, finally shouted at the girl,

> "What the f*** is your problem! You need to get out of my life, I never loved you and never will! I was only with you for the sex!"

The girl replied,

"That's all I wanted to hear..." and left.

The girl moved on finally. Dorian confused stayed awake that night pondering about what had just happened. He thought about everything the girl had done and how her love led her to desperate measures. It was then that Dorian's old feelings surfaced and he realized how much in common he had with her pain. It always amazed me how it took this girl's desperate measures to finally open Dorian's heart again.

Anonymous

Love

I lived and studied in Budapest for 10 years, half of my life. Those were the best 10 years of my life. I was in high school, spending time with my friends, doing every possible type of activity a teenager could do.

It was at a party on what-seemed-then like a regular Friday night where I met Anna. I saw a beautiful brunette girl wearing an elegant black dress. She was talking to one of my friends and I could see she was feeling uncomfortable. My friend, as far as I could tell, was a little drunk and was telling her some stupid things that made her look around the room for an 'escape plan'. She didn't know me then but she recognized my face as we have been going out to the same places for a few months. When she saw me she quickly walked over to me and started talking - just so that the other guy would leave her alone. We started talking and we immediately clicked. I felt like I had to take the opportunity to ask her out then and there because it felt so right (I considered that it might have been the alcohol talking but I had to try regardless). She has been my girlfriend for three years ever since. That exact moment taught me that it isn't a lie when people say, "Do what you think is right". It's not until you experience it that you understand that your first instinct, that feeling that you get, is usually right. After we graduated from high school, it was time for us to head off to universities. She, being Hungarian, applied to a Hungarian university. I on the other hand, applied to the UK.

18+

Before I left, we had an extremely tough choice to make - break up right now or try to have a long distance relationship. I personally was not in favour of a long distance relationship since I felt that it would be hard to keep the same feelings whilst living in different countries. After crying and talking, and more crying, we decided to go ahead and try having a relationship between two countries.

I'm glad to say now that the long distance relationship can really work if both of the people are willing to put effort into it. What we did was set up a schedule of visiting during our holidays. We decided to take turns, like once I would fly to Hungary and once she would fly to London. Another thing that saved our relationship was technology - that's found everywhere nowadays. A high quality webcam and microphone can make you feel almost like you're with each other. We would spend hours on Skype talking to each other just like we were in the same room.

When I was in a new country, an unknown place, an unknown university, I never really felt my best or at home - Like the Kings of Leon might say, "I could really use somebody". Keeping the relationship with my girlfriend kept me happy and sane during my adjustment times in London. What I'm trying to say is, we took a chance and we're happy. A long distance relationship might sound crazy at first, especially when you're a young adult, but it's one of the best choices I ever made.

By Daniel Kaplansky

Pressure and Expectations

We all want to be cool right? To be loved, respected and all

In this part of the book, there are selections of stories which show how sometimes we would do things either because we need to fit in and be seen as normal; or because we want other people to be happy with us.

There will be times when we would change ourselves and abandon who we are; or how we would do things our heart wouldn't tell us to for the pursuit of acceptance and happiness.

There will also be times when we wouldn't be able to cope with the pressures around us; deciding to use harmful and depressing methods of escaping our problems.

In this section, you will realise that if we try to make other people happy and accept us, we can forget about our own happiness too; doing what we want to do to be happy.

Who's the Loser Now?

I knew they were all watching me; they never agreed to what was happening but they never helped me and I hated them all for that. I mean, as long as you don't say anything about an issue and you ignore it—that means you agree with it.

Every Maths lesson I got bullied by Alex and his gang... well it was mostly Alex—his friends just laughed and blurted out unserious exclamations of, "Alright, alright man leave her alone now." But it just encouraged him. He would continue to throw balls of paper at me and scream from the back of the class about what an ugly nerd I was and how happy he was to sit at the back and not see my 'Butters' face. How dumb that word was—stupid English slang. Apparently it meant ugly.

I had just migrated from Antigua and so everything was new to me—the food, the language and not to mention the weather. I had a hard time fitting in because I wasn't sure what to talk about. At lunch time everyone used to talk about music— the latest tracks, the best artists, the liveliest radio stations. The problem was when everyone was talking about Funky House and Grime I couldn't relate—I only listened to Reggae and Dancehall... sometimes a bit of Hip Hop here and there too. I could never talk about that with them... I mean, they wouldn't even understand my accent in the first place much, less to know the music I like. So I was the loser—the super loser with no friends apart from a few shy people that

18+

I was comfortable talking to. It was weird because I was so popular in Antigua... never in a million years I thought I'd be the shy girl that doesn't have friends.

Anyway, I had to stop focusing on how depressing my life was—let's face it, it wasn't going to get me anywhere apart from feeding into how stupid Alex and his entourage of jackasses wanted me to feel. I had GCSEs to worry about—it was already February and exams started in May. I blanked it all out and studied hard, surprisingly the bullying stopped because the idiots were busy studying to fail.

Time flew and before I knew it we had to collect our grades from school. I was confident and decided to open mine in front of everyone—if they hated me I didn't care because I knew I wouldn't see them again. None of them chose the sixth forms (last two years of high school) I had—probably because they knew they would never get in. So it was now the moment of truth. I slipped my fingers under the flap of the envelope—it was so crisp and fresh a bit too easy to open for my liking, I felt a bit uneasy but I still wanted to prove that I was someone... someone that could be something and stand out from the crowd. And so I opened it. I scanned the page and shoved the paper in my bag. I had the biggest, cheekiest grin on my face that pulled everyone towards me. They were all frantically asking,

"Tahira, Tahira what did you get? How did you do?"

I was thinking—oh joy, they know my name. I rolled my eyes and said,

"I got a B..." then I allowed the most painstaking silence before saying:

"And 9 As—can you believe I got a B? I am sooooooo pissed off!"

The looks on their faces were beyond priceless. I felt so good. Even though I really got a mixture of As, Bs and Cs—I made all those people who tried to make my life a nightmare feel as if THEY were in a nightmare. They obviously felt disappointed with their grades and hopefully it pushed them to focus on bettering themselves rather than hurting other people. Well so I hope anyway—I'm just glad I wasn't the loser at the end of the day.

By Tahira

18+

Grades–
the Root Cause of Sorrow in a
Student's Life?

"*Grades do not matter, what matters is the knowledge that you gain whilst preparing for any examination.*" These were the words my favourite teacher had told me when I was preparing for my 10th grade board examination. He was the one who made me realize that board examinations were '*just another set of exams.*' According to him students at least got to know what their grades/marks/percentages secured in these examinations. However, when an individual steps out into the REAL world everyday is an examination for him. He would be scrutinized by the whole world. In this rat-race everyone would look at him and try to figure out even that miniscule fault which would be barely visible! Every individual would have to groom himself and take utmost care about their manners, speech, appearance and habits in public. Even after putting in so much effort the individual would never get to know his grades. No one tells him whether he has passed or failed!

How easily I believed my teacher at that time but now the declaration of the results by the exam boards made me ponder over my teacher's words. Was he really right in saying that marks don't matter? Or was it simply his way to convince me that I should be happy with whatever I score? "*10th grade is a point when you either make or break you future,*" "*If you miss the bus now, you miss it forever,"* words like these pressure the students and make them forget their childhood. Once the student gets promoted to 10th grade his whole life revolves around the set of examinations he has to face and pass 'successfully'!

For them coming second is being first on the list of losers.

This ideology of Ayrton Senna that they are made to believe has prevented them from enjoying their childhood. How often does one see a student playing football or watching Tom and Jerry on the television or reading mindless comics or just simply mucking around? There may be a handful of students who may do a few of these things but a majority of students are forced to study. Going to different tuition classes is all in their day's work. By the time they come back home they are too drained out to even chit-chat with their siblings!

To make matters worse, after putting in so much effort when an average students scores 86% people are unhappy. The whooping percentages (read: 99%) scored by their counterparts adds salt to their injury. Students scoring 90% run around and keep their fingers crossed while trying to get an admission in different colleges, those with 86% think about securing seats through management quota (paid seats)! And those with 81% give up their hopes of getting in a 'good' college. This definition of a 'good' college is highly relative. For a student belonging to the 90%+ category, a 'good' college is much different from the 'good' college of a student who score 75%+!

18+

The result day which is supposed to be the day of happiness for any student has now become a day that they dread! At the end of the day the '*thoda-zyada*' (I-want-more) attitude is responsible for making innumerable students sad. The one scoring 91% thinks about 94% while the one who has scored 85% ponders why he couldn't score 90%. Ever wondered that in this of sea of sadness where one could find a tinge of happiness? Well, it is a student who gets 35% and manages to just pass. The moment he sees 35% on that mark-sheet, his joy knows no bounds. After all, marks do matter, right?

By Gaargi Sharma

School...High School...University...Job?

We have one life to live and that's it, I don't know about an afterlife or second life. I know one thing and that is; this is it, we are born once and we die once in between let's say we have a span of 60 to 65 years at an average. Out of these 65 years at least 20 you spend in school getting valuable knowledge, after that you go to a university and you are there for five years. Followed by 3 years of masters, that's it 28 years gone down the drain or rather taken away. Then the rest you spend working like a dog, so one doesn't have much life left to do what he wants.

Well the reason why I am saying all of this is because I don't believe in the orthodox life cycle set by our fore fathers for us. I had an excellent school life from junior high to high school, one heck of a journey. This is where I start thinking about why the heck do I need to get a university degree if I have to join my father's business. I should focus more on that and learn how it works, get some practical knowledge, according to me book or theory knowledge is only a waste if you don't have the opportunity to have practical experience.

When I left my home and came to university in a different country all together, I was at first very confident of myself. It was just a question of few years, once I am done with the studies I will be back home. And any way I was going to go home for Christmas, so it was only a question of 3 months. Soon I realized that it was not that easy, I started having a lot

18+

of free time on my hand that started to make me feel home sick. I started thinking in an odd way, thinking whether it's even worth me spending time here and wasting money behind it.

I started thinking I would rather leave education for good and go back to India and start working with my father and get trained by him. Now that idea of mine was not acceptable by the rest. However, after months of talks and discussion with my parents, I finally convinced them to look at an option where I could go back and continue studying in a college in Mumbai and work with dad as well and understand the business.

Somehow after a lot of effort it didn't work out, which I kind of expected the answer to be. They told me the only option now was for me to finish the rest of my course out here. My dad had a set idea of what he wanted me to do and that was what I had to follow. Strangely you would always feel that you are selecting what you want to do but it is always influenced by one of your loved ones. In my case my father influenced most of my decisions.

I have started to live with the situation because I have no other option and am making the best of what I can do. Although I would always tell people, don't select to go out because of any influence only if it is going to do good for you then make a call. Don't let someone else decide for you whether it is good or bad to go to a university away from home. If you are old enough to stay alone in another country then you certainly old enough to decide on your own. Respect everyone's opinion but follow your own brain and heart.

By Raheel Shah

My Silly Pursuit of What I Thought Would Matter...

The worse thing that could happen in a test/exam is that you thought you got the solution when actually it's not. If you thought you got the solution, you will probably not think twice about whether it's correct or not. So in the event that it's not, basically you are screwed because throughout the entire duration of the test/exam, you are having the false hope that you got it right and it's not going to be a nice outcome. Moreover, if you write the correct answer and then change it thinking that it is wrong, the feeling could be worse!

Well, that happened to me just now during the Chemistry test. I wouldn't say that it was disastrous, yet it would suffice to say that I am not satisfied with my performance as I have allowed complacency to get the better of me.

Having said that, it should be noted that my little mistake will probably not affect my grade by much. Yet, I have somehow allowed this little issue to affect my mood and I sulked my way home. It was only halfway throughout the bus ride that the reason for such undesirable action dawned upon me.

I have been stressing myself too much this semester, despite the fact that I hardly study! God only knows why I get so stressed! I guess I am stressed because I want to be close to perfection. I tried too hard, in my silly pursuit for perfection.

It's ironic, that in my silly pursuit to perfection, I have inevitably revealed my imperfections in character. And in that silly pursuit of what I thought would matter, I have neglected so many things in life including friends, family, fun and my health. It is only in this semester that I realized this!

I have neglected my friends. I have rejected outing invites, I have failed to initialize lunch with a good friend and I have neglected certain groups of friends all in the name of "*I need to study*". But of course, I never end up studying. All I do is procrastinate!

I have neglected my family. I didn't keep my of helping out my mum in her work and I have not really spoken to them for quite a long time, all in the name of *"I need to study".*

I became selfish and self-centred in my pursuit of the dreams which I thought would matter if I achieved them. Even after achieving that, will I then be happy? Our wants are endless, after achieving this one, there will be another and another. When will we then ever be satisfied? I failed to see that I ought to be satisfied with what I have, and not to be dejected with what I don't. It's quite sad that it took me so long to learn to appreciate things around me; I am such an ingrate I realized.

For now, I feel that I should just try my best in the things I do and not to be so concerned with exams and grades for they do not define who I am. People assess you based on you, not

(18+)

your grades. These thoughts will probably end my silly pursuit of what I thought mattered!

Anonymous

Hope – a 2-Edged Sword

The word "hope" generally has very positive connotations to it. Most of the time when we are totally down and helpless, we can only live in hoping that everything turns out right. It gives us strength to carry on working. It doesn't matter if the odds are against us.

I am sure that we've all encountered times when the situation is dire and there doesn't seem to be a way out: exams coming but feeling unprepared, mortgage assignments due but no idea how to do it, etc. But yet, despite all of this, we continue to strive - continue to study hard, hoping that by some stroke of luck, what we read two seconds before stepping into the exam hall will miraculously come out; that the stock market suddenly picks up, that the assignment's solution will suddenly strike our head. Yes, hope generally is a good thing. It keeps us doing the things we really want to do.

Yet when what we hope for doesn't come through, we will feel disappointed. The more hope that we have, the more disappointment we will potentially feel. Sometimes, it is best just not to hope for anything at all. Wouldn't that make us all satisfied with our lives? If we don't hope for a good life, we won't feel so shitty about ourselves even if our life turned out to be all screwed up. Ok, maybe not, but we'll feel less shitty perhaps. If we didn't hope that we would get into an Ivy League College with full Scholarship, then we wouldn't feel disappointed if we get a 50% scholarship. If we didn't hope

18+

that we would get an A+ for the assignment, we wouldn't feel bitter if we got a B. if we didn't hope that our friends will be nice to us, we wouldn't be sad if they changed.

Well, perhaps I might be getting a little mixed up with hope and expectation here, but I think there's a really fine line between both. Generally, I think that hope slowly becomes expectation (and probably vice versa). For instance, in university context: we start off by hoping to get a perfect GPA and because of that we get down to working hard. Due to the hard work that we've put in, the hope of getting a perfect GPA slowly becomes an expectation of getting a perfect GPA. Then when we don't get a perfect score and get a 4.3 instead of 4.5 GPA we feel sad!!

I think in general, it's good to hope but not to have too much of it. The big difficulty is trying to find the right balance, innit??

Anonymous

The Art of Happiness

When I was young, I was told by my mother that if I studied hard and got into college I would be happy.

Well when I did get into college, I found I was happy since I worked hard to pass, but now I had to work harder and take more lessons and coursework. I wasn't happy for long, I was stressed!

My mother then told me one night, "Well it's all about getting into university. Do that and then you'll be happy". I took on what she said and two years later, I achieved one of the highest grades in my class which allowed me to go into a top university.

I was happy!!!

But then all of a sudden, I had more work than I ever had in my life! More coursework, projects and on top if that, I had to get a job to help with my rent and bills since I lived out.

I was tired of all this promise of happiness which doesn't last very long.

I predicted what was gonna happen next: mum would say, get a masters degree and then you'll be happy. Haha!

And then once you have that, get a good job and then you'll be happy.

(18+)

It's not just in education however, relationships for example: I managed to ask out a girl I've known for years. I was over the moon when she accepted. It wasn't long before she tried to change me and impose on my life.

I would always make money but for some reason it would faster leave me than it came to me.

I sometimes wondered if we can ever have happiness which can last forever instead of those false promises that is offered by everything around us.

The truth is, I don't know the answer. So one day I asked my uncle, "What do you think we should do to be happy?"

He said to me, "Nothing at all."

I stared perplexed and confused.

He continued, "We always want things in life and suddenly when we get them, we get that happy feeling. Soon we start to lose that feeling because its old news and we want something else to make us happy again, it's a never ending cycle. When you finally stop wanting, you become free."

I felt something meaningful in his statement and was going to explore it, but then he picked up his whiskey and I remembered he was an alcoholic.

I believe that the problem lies in knowing what you want and need. I don't remember any games or cars that kept me happy very long, but I always remember being happy when I'm with my true friends and family. When I think about them, my happiness rarely goes away.

By Tung Nguyen

(18+)

Convenient Conclusions...
Haste is Waste!

It has become our habit to jump to conclusions without even ascertaining the facts and evidence. Somehow, we assume things and believe what we want to believe, irrespective of the facts. If you heard about a student jumping from the top of a building and committing suicide, you would conveniently state- might be because of his break up or maybe because he failed this semester! So, when you see the news on the ever-vigilant media, you want to tell everyone and yourself – see, I told you so. Even if evidence to the contrary is presented to you on a platter and it is proved that he committed suicide for some other reasons, you just won't believe it. '*I'm sure the police have been suitably bribed by the University and the case will be hushed up now.*'

How convenient!

There's an accident on the road and you see a motor-cyclist lying bleeding on the road. There's a car driver standing and waiting for the police to come. He's trying to get in touch with his office, friends and family to tell them what happened. Slowly but surely, the mob starts to grow and there's palpable tension in the air. Without ascertaining the facts of the case and without checking who actually was at fault, someone says, 'These people are such rash drivers. Who do they think they are? These rich snobs!' Suddenly, there's someone in the crowd, for his own reasons, ready to take out his angst against the car-driver. Nobody is bothered about taking the injured to the hospital and everyone is just enjoying the drama. The driver is vainly trying to tell anyone who is willing to listen, that the motorbike was driving rashly and was at fault or jumped the red light causing accident, but who is there to listen to him? If he's rich, he must have exploited poor; if he's a poor under-dog, he can't be wrong!

Once again, it is so convenient to believe in the stereotype, isn't it?

Imagine if you see a beautiful car and the person driving it happens to be nattily dressed and lo! You conclude that he must be the paid driver – even if the facts are contrary to this. He is probably the owner, but hello? You cannot be wrong! You meet someone at the University's Orientation party in China and that person is wearing an expensive watch or diamonds. If the person seems to be well dressed and wealthy, you conclude that the watch/diamonds must be real; otherwise, a poorly dressed person is assumed to be wearing 'fake' Rolex.

This is not limited to the whole wealth and 'I-am-rich-you-are-not' thing. If you see a young couple coming from the opposite direction holding hands, you immediately reach a conclusion that they must be boyfriend and girlfriend. Ah! And what if it is an old man with a young girl – he must be her sugar-daddy and if they are simply two men together –GAY!

(18+)

And so on. We don't even bother to consider that they may be brother-sister, dad-daughter or good friends!

Many-a-times, what we assume turns out to be correct, thereby re-enforcing the stereotypes in our minds. And this thing has happened with me as well. Lost my I-pod charger: Someone stole it. Lost my TOK book: Abhimanyu is irresponsible, he cannot take care of my book. At other times, we're proved wrong. But, by using our *'selective perception'* sub-consciously, we ignore this as a mere exception. We continue to believe what we want to believe. But how long will it make you feel 'good' about yourself? I say- not so long. Someday you will have to come out and accept the reality. Never jump on convenient conclusions! Never!

Are we too lazy to jump to convenient conclusions with ascertaining facts or are plainly prejudiced by our up-bringing, education and circumstances?

Anonymous

18+

Family, Friends and Religion

Family Friends and religion, are the three main pillars of life,
these are the basic foundation that develops who we are.

Incidents involving family or friends can change
one's life forever; changes for the good or for bad.

We do things in our life that is influenced by the family,
friends and religion. Many people are vegetarian because
of their religion and many don't like spending time
with family since they have had a bad experience.

These situation, circumstances and
incidents help us to be who we are.

Here are some stories that would reveal an incident that
took place in teenage life and changed the person for ever.

Life is Not Fair, Why?

When I was young I always thought everything ends with a good ending just like any good storybook. I guess I was wrong. Around the age of 10, I had developed an idea that someone whom we loved or were very close to would never leave you and go, will always be by your side. That was all a lie...

All of this came to an abrupt end. On the 20th December 2008, 3:15 Am in the morning my grandfather took his last breath and that was it. He left and he went to a place that no one can ever get him back from.

I will never forget that night, my grandfather was not well for quite some time, he was suffering from cancer, we had initially treated him in 2004 and he did just fine until mid September 2008, when it all came back. He stopped eating and his health started to decline. He started to complain about having double vision and so we consulted our family doctor as well as the leading neurologists. They told us there was a possibility that the cancer had reached his brain.

As soon as we could get all the results and conclusions, we started him on the medication. While all this was going on, I was in London studying not knowing a single thing. My family had decided to keep me in the dark, since they were worried that I might not be able to deal with it. As time passed by his health started to get worse and his friend in London could not keep it from me and so revealed everything to me. At that time with my luck, I could take a week off due to a reading week in my university and spend all that time with my grandfather. At that point it seemed he was doing well.

Then started the worst time of all that November, he was shifted to the hospital where his health was declining on an hourly basis; the time was rough and he was not responding. He was put on a life support system for one night and the doctors gave him 2 hours to live. My family didn't know what to do, whether to call me or not. With some miracle he recovered and everything was fine; the next day my dad called me and informed me. Since then whenever I received a call I used to tremble to pick up the phone, not knowing what would come and just blow me out. For the first time I could hear fear in my dad's voice, a man I never saw trembling had lost his confidence. He needed me, I needed to be with my grandfather.

I still precisely remember on the 5th of December my grandfather called me and just spoke two words, "Come back," I sought help from my group members, finished a project early and landed in India by the 11th of December. From the time I landed not one day did I leave my grandfather's side; I was with him day and night. I could not bear seeing his pain, I used to cry myself to sleep to see him in the situation he was in.

Who knew what was around the corner, on the 19th December, my friends called me and told me to come out for

(18+)

dinner. It would cheer me up since I had not left home since I had landed. So I did go, at around 9:00 PM when I sat for dinner and was about to order, my mom calls me and tells me to reach home at any cost. I got scared, terrified, and drove like a maniac back home not following a single driving rule. Upon my arrival, I was informed that there was a possibility that cancer might have spread to my grandfather's kidney and that doctors were going to do some tests. The test results arrived by 1:00 in the morning of 20th December, that whole night till around 2:30, I was sitting next to him. At 3:00 I decided to go up and take some sleep. At 3:15 my grandfather took his last breath, he passed away. The nurse informed my dad there was something wrong, and on hearing that he ran down followed by my mother. At 3:30 we had the doctor pronounce him dead.

All this while I was sleeping I didn't know what was happening. At 4:00 my mom bangs my door and tells me to come out. As soon as I answered the door she told me, "Dada is no more." My ears went numb I didn't know how to react. I was stiff; it was as if someone had just kicked me hard in my balls. I rushed down and there I saw my grandma in tears my father, in tears and my grandfather lying there with a piece of white cloth on him. I was trying to say something, words were just not coming out of my mouth, I was in a state of shock, didn't understand a single thing that was happening around me.

In our religion we cremate the body and as a grandson I was an essential part of the ritual. I saw my grandfather's body in the furnace and could never get over that. The man who I knew with pride, honour, dignity, respect, and enormous amount of love from around him was no longer amongst us.

My problem started a month after this, I started dreaming about him and started thinking that he was trying to talk to me, trying to tell me something and as the days passed by, I developed insomnia. I lost my sleep at night, didn't know what to do, at first I used to run away from the situation. The situation increased to a level where I lost sleep completely, so I thought that it was time to talk to someone. I spoke to my aunt one evening and then I spoke with my mother. They both suggested, "Give it time." It did work to an extent and after some time I started to move on. There are still times when I wonder and get lost in the same situation. One thing I learned from my grandfather was that whatever life is there, live it to the largest, it is given only once and so enjoy it.

He always said this during his treatment for cancer:

"I have lived my first innings of life successfully, and now live the s second innings."

By Raheel Shah

18+

Self Respect

I used to know this one guy, we went to the same secondary school together and we were in the same maths class. He was much popular and cooler than me and I was just a geek at the time (In fact I still am!!), we became very good friends and I got to know a lot of cool people thanks to him. But he had his downside: he would always ask me for money, ask to come over, eat my food, sometimes he would sleepover, and even sleep on my bed!! (While I slept on the floor!) He would do this for a few months and it was really beginning to frustrate me. Then when everyone started telling me that he was just taking advantage of me, I couldn't take it anymore. One school day when it came to home time, he chased me to the school gate and asked to come over; I finally stood up to him and told him that he couldn't stay over any more. He gave a very sad look and was like "oh ok," saying bye and walked to his house in the other direction which was 5 minutes away compared to mine which was 30 minutes on bus!

After that, school days weren't the same, he wouldn't talk to me as much, we hung out less and I felt isolated, but at least I took control against being taken advantage off...right?

Maybe I should have let him continue to use me. Maybe he didn't even realize what he was doing that because I never said anything.

All I know is that I was down a friend, but in return, I felt I had more control over my life and gained more respect from that.

I made new friends now, they're fun and I enjoy my time with them. Sometimes when they step over the line, I would tell him how I feel and they're fine with it. We move on and stay as friends.

By Tung Nguyen

(18+)

My Dog

It was my 10th birthday when my parents surprised me with a small poodle. She was peach coloured, playful with people, hated other dogs and was always very jealous if she wasn't getting attention. Her name was Pitsi, meaning tiny in Hungarian. Throughout winter she would play with my siblings and I in the snow, running through it when it was the highest and shaking it off when she finally got out. In the summer she would play with us in the garden, chasing us around in return for a little tummy scratch. Since I can remember every night when I took my socks off before going to bed, she would run into my room and bring them back to her sleeping pillow.

As we both got older we played outside less and even though she was always loyal following me around I would pat her less and less. One day I came home and realized how faded and thin her fur became. What used to be thick, bright ripe peach coloured coat, turned into thinning curly peach fuzz fur. It also became apparent that she was really skinny and would barely eat dog food. Although this was most likely a trick to get us to finally feed her people food, it still made her look very aged. But it seemed no matter how old she looked, when I called her name, 'Pitsi!' she would run faster than most dogs I know and jump on to get patted.

Due to a condition which causes me to have very dry eyes, I would always manually rub them to get them to water a bit.

With this condition I would always wash my hands constantly in order to not infect my eyes. These two factors also caused me to pat Pitsi less as each time I would have to wash my hands and she would keep coming to me to keep patting her. As we grew more distant and I moved on to university she became more attached to my mom. She would follow her around the house and sit next to her at the dinner table. But no matter what, if I shouted, 'Pitsi!' she would come with her tongue out with what always looked like a doggy smile on her face.

It was the day that I flew back home to visit my friends and family that I will always remember. I took a taxi home from the airport because my family was returning from a vacation and hadn't arrived yet. I unlocked the door and turned on the lights. To my horror I found Pitsi lying on top of the couch on her back just twitching and having muscle spasms. She looked possessed and I just ran to her. She was foaming and drooling from her mouth and urinating uncontrollably. Then all of a sudden she stopped with her back arched and all four of her legs strained with flexed muscles in different directions. The indication that I had that she was still alive was her eye following me. It looked like she was in so much pain and I couldn't do anything; her muscles were contracted as hard as her brain could make them. I slowly tried to massage her legs and turn her around. Finally, she let up and was back to normal. She was so helpless in the matter and it was agonizing watching her trying recapture herself. Finally my mom arrived home. She witnessed this seizure happen again before we could finally take her to the vet. Once there, the

18+

vet gave us medicine to give her. We took her home but she looked sickly and miserable. Everything seemed new to her as she would drag herself around the house smell everything like she'd never seen it before. When I called out, 'Pitsi!' she didn't even react. We spent most of our time taking turns holding her and making sure she felt comfortable. Once again she would have the seizure whilst walking up the stairs, causing her to fall down. We took her to the vet again who only finally took us seriously after she had her heartbreaking fit in front of him. My parents prepared all of us for death and made us all say our good-byes. The vet finally determined after many tests that a she had something wrong with her spinal nerves. He prescribed a different type of medicine and filled her up with pain killers.

That day she came home with us as if nothing ever happened. She ran around the house with her tongue out, cheery and happy. Answered to her name again and didn't leave us alone for a second to lie down. In my head she was going to live for forever and I would never have to go through the trauma again. I was relaxed and happy knowing I would never have to be exposed to watching her suffer without understanding of what's happening, until a week later when it got worse. She had another seizure again, urinating herself again, foaming at the mouth again and having her muscles bend her head back and muscles in different directions. Pitsi could only control her watery eyes that would follow you as you tried to help. We had to take her quickly to the vet who finally put her to sleep. I was depressed that my two siblings got a picture with her before she was put to sleep. I figured I'm a young adult and I would be able to take losing a pet, which I did for a week. I told my friends about it and they were all sad for me, but I didn't shed a tear. A week later I came home late on a Saturday night, I took my socks off and threw them into the corner of the room. It was finally seeing a miserable pile of socks that caused my eyes to tear up, and I cried until I fell asleep.

I was depressed for a week but when I finally cried everything felt better. I learned that night that letting your emotions goes sometimes is the best cure when you're feeling down. It's been several months since she passed away. I usually talk about her like she is still alive but with time you learn to deal with it.

By Bar Segal

18+

Move On!!

For the first time in life I felt that moving on is a big thing, and if one does not decide to move on and live in the past, there would be many things that he would miss out in life. My family and I were traveling to our temple in a place in Gujarat, the place is around 100 Km from Ahemdabad, which one has to travel by car. On the way their you get to see some parts of rural India, which always puts me into thoughts of "how can one leave like this?" why is it that some have it and some don't.

I always wonder how amongst this gigantic mountains and magnificent bed of green grass lays a fact that we want to cover and not look at. The poverty in India: People suffering from hunger, disease that they cannot afford to cure and so they have to see their loved ones die. I feel helpless when I see such things and can't don anything about it. It pains me that I have so much money and it is not good enough to help others around me.

When I was at my temple rejuvenating spiritually, mentally and physically, I was thinking about all of these things that one hesitates to think about. It is then that I saw the real horror of life; a lady approached my family, and me, she had never met us nor heard about us nor had we. She started to talk to us saying that she needed help, desperate help she told us that she was suffering from HIV and her husband was also suffering. She was certain she was going to die and didn't have enough days to leave. She had a son who was 4 years old. All she wanted to do was to secure her son's future, and make sure there is someone to look after him and pay for his needs.

I could not handle myself; a drop of tear fell on my hand and made me feel shit on inside. I wanted to do everything possible to help that lady and her family. I spoke to my father and made sure that she would be assisted with help at the NGO, with funds and medication that is required. We took her contact details and spoke to the head of the NGO to look into the matter and help in whatever way possible.

From all of this I learnt one thing, birth and death is not in our hands. One must enjoy his life completely and at the same time spend time with his loved ones not feeling guilty of missing out on something. I feel as if I have missed out on lot and have been stuck in past. I learnt that I have to forget of what has happened in past and I have to move on to enjoy what is coming ahead, and what is planned for me. I have to be strong and face it in life. I learnt that I cannot run away from it, it's not the right thing to do, deal with it. I am crying over certain losses after enjoying the time with those people, I can't even imagine of what the kid would go through for knowing the he would be losing both his parents. I can't imagine what his parents would be feeling about dyeing and not being able to fulfill the needs of their son. I have to live in today and enjoy it to the max. I have learnt that, remember things to cherish them but don't live in them, move on.

Raheel Shah

(18+)

Paying a Price for Being Too Kind eh?

Every time when your so-called friend approaches you for some work, you are stuck in a dilemma. You don't know what to do! Should I say 'Yes' or should simply be curt and turn down the request by saying a harsh 'No'? You must have noticed that I didn't call the person my 'friend'. Instead I referred to the person as a so-called friend because if that person were a real friend he/she would have never asked you a 'favour' when that individual knows how busy you are!

Some time back, there was this guy whom I befriended in the school library. He approached me for help on some chemistry questions. Now, firstly, I was surprised that he chose me! Our library is so freaking big (the biggest single floored library in Asia!) with so many students cramming their work; I only wondered why, of all people, he chose me. I don't have an "I-am-smart-Come-here-for-free chemistry-consultation" tag on me, do I?

However, being a kind person, I responded to him with an affirmative nod and helped him to solve almost every question that was on that sheet. I put aside my own problems for more than an hour. Now, I have no problem with that, in fact, he gave me an opportunity to revise my stuff. It's what that happened after this incident that annoyed me. Since then, he began bugging me almost every day, and yes, I was dumb enough to give him my cell number.

The point is, I have absolutely nothing against helping people. But I was disgusted with this particular guy for his persistence. I had my own stuff to be done and I guess he forgot that my world does not revolve around him and his problems. Or was I the only person he could turn to? Even my friends noticed it and some even made fun of me asking me if he's my boyfriend or something. Damn! Wished I could have just told him off, but hey, my heart says that I just didn't wanna hurt his feelings.

Instead, I gave subtle hints that I wished to be left alone, like not replying to his unrelenting texts and avoiding him in class. But he just didn't seem to get it. That is the price one has to pay for being too kind. One should never pretend to be friendly with the person you are uncomfortable with. Pretend for what? In the end both suffered. How? Well, eventually I had gathered the courage to go up to him and speak my mind. It must have hurt him but I had no other choice. One suggestion for all you guys and girls reading this- never try to be too polite and too kind. You might just end up hurting yourselves!

Anonymous

(18+)

Once Upon A Time

Once upon a time in a season full of sun and sleep, I thought I was living in a perfect world where everything revolved around me. Little did I know that whatever goes up must eventually come crashing down.

I took my vacation time as cavalier as I could; I went out all the time and spent all my money on things I couldn't remember the next day. Stories I heard about myself day after day started to sound more and more twisted. I heard them from people I didn't know and especially from people I didn't want to hear them from. I tried to hide from my mistakes and the choices I made, but they always seemed to know where I was going. In the broad daylight everyone around me seemed to know my biggest secret of all. I tried to be as conspicuous as I could, but everything I had done in the past only ran faster and faster after me.

Like any idiot teenager, I figured since my problems were catching up with me, I would just run faster too. I literally ran away from all my problems and hid myself behind empty bottles of alcohol and sex. I kept going and going until I literally found myself with nowhere else to go. I couldn't go back home since it was the first place I ran away from, and I couldn't go to anyone I knew because it was the most embarrassing thing I could ever have committed. I just hid myself from myself. I kept pretending that I was okay and I was doing all the right things. I thought I could keep this up and survive my entire life this way; not having a home, any money, or anyone for that matter.

It was the stupidest thing I've ever done.

To be honest, to cut the story in half, I literally became too exhausted to try to survive each and every day. I stumbled home by myself and feared the worst that could possibly happen.

I rang the doorbell in the middle of the night and let myself into my room where there was nothing but dust around. The room was dark and lonely and I just sunk into a sleep that I didn't want to leave for days.

Of course though, in the morning, my Dad woke me and all of the problems I tried to escape from obviously caught up with me in the most violent of ways. He said he did everything because he loved me, whether it had been too much love or just not enough. I still know what I did and what I put myself through. I wouldn't go back to change any of it, I wouldn't go back and have done things differently. It was the worst thing I've ever done, the worst feeling I've ever felt, but it's something that everyone has to understand - in their own way of course. Everyone has to go through their ultimate lows and get back up and just know that there will be people on the other side waiting there to love you.

And you can't always run away from your problems. Because no matter how fast you run, life will always catch

18+

up with you when you do. Home is where the heart is, and whether you know it or not, home will never leave you.

BY KG

Loving Yourself First

A couple of years back, I watched a very old Japanese film. It had been a long time so I had forgotten the title of the film, but it was a story about two brothers and how they grew up with strict parents around the time of the war between China and Japan.

The older brother, Shinji, was very smart and talented two and the younger brother, Hiro, was also smart but he was the youngest so his parents paid little attention to him since he wasn't the successor of the family.

Suddenly the older, Shinji, catches a fatal illness and although he recovers afterwards, he loses his voice in the process. From then on, he is seen as different and intelligently incapable in the eyes of both his parents and society in that time. Everyone turns their attention to Hiro and makes him the successor of the family. Shinji still achieves high scores in school but his family pay little attention. The rest of the film focuses on the brothers' fight to win their parents' acceptance and love. Shinji, continually shun and rejected by his parents, eventually becomes depressed and in the end, feeling no worth in the world, Shinji hangs himself.

This film stayed with me for a long time because I could relate to it so well.

(18+)

There have been many times as a youngster, where I would do things to gain other people's acceptance, to become cool and part of the crowd, to gain the respect of my uncles by being who they wanted me to be.

In the long run, it didn't work out. I wasn't happy with what I was doing and I didn't like the friends I made from being someone else, and if I did something different, they would give me a funny look like, "You're different." There never seemed to be acceptance when I showed my true side.

It's a shame that kids have to put themselves through so much pressure to do well in school so they can gain acceptance by their parents.

Same with relationships I've had, they would always try to change me, from my fashion to my outlook on life. They didn't love me for who I was, they loved me for what they wanted me to be.

I realised that it's best to gain the love and acceptance of yourself first. To embrace your odd habits and personality, and cultivate and cherish your positive sides. So that even when the world abandons you, you will never abandon yourself.

Shinji hated himself because he never accepted himself, he worked hard for others to accept him but his inability to speak made him seem different and that was hard to bear.

By Tung Nguyen

Frienemy

This story takes place some time ago. I do not remember the exact timing, maybe because I forgot or maybe because I just don't want to.

Still an awkward kid trying to fit in a new school, it's not easy, especially when you don't even speak the language. I guess that's what drew me so close to Collin. Collin and I both came from the same country and we were both new at school. I was better at English than he was so I was his assigned as his friend to help him understand this new environment. We became best friends shortly after.

Always hanging out before school, in school, and after school I would go to his house or he would come to mine. Maybe it's because I did not have many friends that I didn't notice this, but all Collin was, was a bully. He would make me do things for him like his homework or folding his clothes, he would make me pay for things and he really would never care about how I felt.

I remember one time we were both far away from our houses and we needed to take a taxi. He said, "I'm not paying for a taxi home!" He knew that as it got darker, he would leave me no choice but to pay for the taxi. He also knew that I only had enough money to take a taxi to his house, which would mean I'd have to walk home the rest of the way. Another day we would sit in his house I would watch him play computer. When I wanted a turn he wouldn't let me and when I wanted a drink he wouldn't let me. These things would constantly happen and I would not even realize how much of a jerk he was. I didn't even realize it when my mother drove us somewhere one day and he told me, "Move over, fat pig!" It only hit me after my mother started scolding him,

"That is very rude Collin! Especially to a friend!"

"What? He IS a pig..."

It occurred to me all of a sudden. My brain flashed all the bad things he has done to me over the years: the lunch money he would take from me, the detention he got me in and all the times I caught him wiping boogers on my back.

Getting out of that car, I don't know what came over me. It was an out of body experience. I felt my stomach boiling with anger, my mind working in a million thoughts per second, my eyes watery from all the emotion and soon enough my fist clenched closed. I pulled and with all my force I swung my right hand towards his face. That day was the first time I broke a bone. As he dodged my hand and it went flying into a wall, I could hear the crack in my wrist and my fingers. I screamed like a little girl. Collin just stared and asked, "What the hell was that for you idiot!" Even in agonizing pain he still never understood.

Since that day I haven't spoken a word to him. With a fractured bone, I met lots of new people in school and made lots of new friends. Collin was mostly alone until he finally left to another school. I'm not going to lie, it did make me happy seeing him friendless.

The point I'm getting at is: don't be stupid, open your eyes and see who your real friends are. Getting hurt by a friend hurts more than anything. Being in an abusive relationship can only end badly.

By Anonymous

18+

Blessed

When I was young, I used to spend a lot of my time with my grandma. She didn't have a lot of company and my parents were always working, so they used to leave me with her for the whole day.

There wasn't much to do at my grandma's. The shops were far away, the neighbours were quiet and the area was generally peaceful. Something I didn't really appreciate back then.

What I did love to do however, was to read, and when my grandma found out, she explained that she was a Christian and lent me the bible to read just to see what it was like.

The bible was complicated, full of chapters and words I didn't understand. However, I understood the story of Adam and Eve and Noah's Ark, something I heard in school and read about in books many times during nursery.

I didn't really find the bible interesting at all and was about to give up on it until I came across a quote from a page which took my attention.

> "Speak up for those who cannot speak for themselves, for the rights of all who are destitute."

This quote was found in Proverbs 31:8.

I didn't understand the word destitute so I asked my grandma about it and she told me destitute meant weak, poor and in need of help. Many people are poor in the world and many of them want help, but cannot receive help. Many of them are forced to do things they don't like and many live in fear every second of their lives.

The quote above really touched me because there was something very noble and humane about standing up for the defenceless. To defend those who can't defend themselves for whatever reason.

My heart poured out to them and I felt the need to continue reading the bible to understand more.

From then on, the proverbs from the bible were my best friend. Something about this advice and wisdom really touched me and I felt as if the words were reaching into my heart.

There were many other words from though I was young, I felt like I understood them very well because they made sense.

In Proverbs 11:13-

"A Gossip betrays a confidence, but the trustworthy keeps a secret."

Or Proverbs 12:25

"Anxiety weighs down the heart, but a kind

18+

word cheers it up."

Proverbs 12:20

"Deceit is in the hearts of those who plot evil,
but those who promote peace have joy."

I was so intrigued and inspired that I asked my grandma if I could borrow the bible, she happily agreed and I also started going to church. Later on I decided to start taking up on holy communions and bible studies.

That was many years ago as a child.

Now these powerful wise words and advice from our Lord still lives in me today. I am blessed to have been given these lessons early on for they have allowed me to walk the path of righteousness and peace, as well as stopped me from taking any paths which would have led me down to evil and to the destruction of my heart, mind and soul.

Anonymous

Personal Journal

Dear Future Me

Prologue

The file is a letter written on the 10th of October 2009 and sent via Futureme.org to myself on the 11th of November 2009. It contains bits of a variety of my journal entries over 9 months of my 18 year old life that I considered valuable.

Ruth Pinto

Dear Future Me,

It's been under a month since I wrote my previous letter and it bothers me that I can't read it as and when I choose. I've become so used to reading my journal that it's become my comfort. I need to keep rewinding and figuring out when I felt what, and how and why. Yet the manner in which I analyse my writings is worrying and rather similar to that of conducting a study on the self.

It's a strange sort of dependency. I never thought I'd need my journal. The purpose of keeping one was merely to reinforce things I'd learned during the day, and to put words to what I thought, and how I felt, and my reactions to various situations. It was meant to help me understand myself and reinforce who I was and who I wanted to be. I never thought I'd keep such writings for extensive periods of time, I never thought I'd need to. I did think I'd occasionally flip through them, but that was only to remind myself of whom I was and who I am now.

It's been a few years since 'journal entries' became a habit. I don't know if being dependent on them is okay. I'm a minimalist who fears emotional dependency, making this need problematic. My writings are me in a sense. Then again, they are my own account of my past self (just as these thoughts have been written much before you began reading them). Isn't it important to let go in order to move forward?

18+

(Just in case writing this leads to me destroying my journals in an attempt to move forward, here are a few bits of what you wrote and how you felt at various points of time during the last couple of months it's a lot more than I previously believed, so take your time with it):

13/02/09

Passion is a brilliant gift. Once you figure out how to tap into this passion and what drives you and gives you joy, everything becomes possible. Everybody is filled with this gift, but it is only once we become passionate people that the world becomes a joyous place, and love will conquer.

24/02/09

It's important to learn to accept not just situations and their consequences, but your own emotional reactions to them. If something upsets you, let it. For only if you accept the way you truly feel and permit yourself to experience that emotion in its entirety, can you discover yourself and adapt accordingly.

26/03/09

I thought I had conquered my fear, but once again, all I had done was look it in the face and then push it aside.

I need to become it to destroy it. And it is just that thought that is so frightening.

01/05/09

I'm sorry about the way things have taken a turn. I wish, for your sake, they weren't so. At times like these, it is more important than ever for you to remember to love, to give. That is one gift you have that no one else can control or take away from you. It is also the one thing that can keep you sane and moving, and rescue you. Don't ever forget that.

09/05/09

I missed you, but I taught myself to forget. It was easier to think of and for myself. I became absorbed in what I convinced myself was a lot, but was honestly not enough.

Of late I've begun to stay away from people. Noise has become a synonym for their general presence. It's so much easier this way; I've convinced myself of my happiness. I can live with just my books and sunrises. Who needs a world full of people lacking passion? All I want is peace - my perception of this notion.

19/05/09

We're human, we care.

25/05/09

The rock was still warm from the kisses of the day's sun. Some dried fish that escaped the women's baskets filled the air with their new found scent; the birds were dozing amongst the sleeping leaves of the watchful trees, as the fishermen heaved their vessels back and forth through the frothy waves.

The stars began to gather as I prayed. I let my voice carry for them all to hear. They listened, they watched, while I cried.

It was a night whose serenity and comfort I needed and for which I shall forever be grateful.

13/06/09

'I wish a lot of things didn't and hadn't and weren't.'

To trust the things people did, and the souls they were before you know them can sometimes be difficult. Yet wishing it were any easier can bring about nothing good or remotely productive. The only thing worth wishing for here is the courage and ability to accept.

22/06/09

You are as confounding as they come. I have never known anyone who favours simplicity to be so complicated. Other than me, that is.

29/06/09

Maybe I deserve more.

09/07/09

There are times when certain moments determine how you live a day. There are days that flow well, stimulate enough endorphins to keep you smiling, and refuse to let your mind settle on negative thoughts.

Today should be a good day. Everything seems to be forward moving, everything but me.

There are things that are happening, things on my mind that I cannot ignore. They're pulling me down, and it's difficult to believe that something so uplifting can become so heavy on the mind.

I'm a soul that needs understanding with reference to myself. I need to know where I stand; it's no longer just a want. I dislike the situation I'm in. For once, I wish things were different. I wish I didn't have to deal with all of this. Up until now, I was happy with the way things were, with all I had learned and shared and become a part of. It's not that I want things to go back to the way they were, I just wish to move forward.

The evening seems to have its effects.

11/07/09

Plan: it is essential. Don't wait; give in to your needs and aspirations. There is so much to do, and there will never be enough time. The least you can do is try. Give love and the world a chance.

(18+)

22/07/09

There's much I haven't thought about in a while. Whether I've done so out of fear of being trapped by such thoughts or because I simply don't think that way anymore, I do not know.

It's time to rewind and move forward.

I don't think this is something I want anymore. I apologise for giving you any sort of hope that I would be strong enough to see this through. I had hoped I would be too.

23/07/09

Brilliant food, music, books, and company can help turn things around a lot more effectively than I previously believed. I may still be as lost and confused and tired as before, but I'm happy. Very happy.

25/07/09

Turns out my family are my ticket out of this sort of stupor. They are simply excellent.

27/07/09

I don't know if I can do this, if I can start again without having to forget.

30/07/09

On that narrow street, change was a constant; now change is a conscious decision. It might have brought with it surprise and pain, but I still wish to embrace it, just as I always have.

02/08/09

I've never known change more intimately. Its ability to help me understand myself is incredible.

It's easier now to let go and let things take whatever course they choose. I'm not waiting for an explanation, or apology. In fact, I'm not waiting at all. I've become a bit preoccupied with understanding the world.

05/08/09

Nothing is unattainable or impossible. All you need to acknowledge is that you have control over nothing other than yourself. If you master yourself, all is mastered.

Changing the way you view things is essential in conquering them. Things might exist as they are, but we see and perceive them as we are. Therefore, in our attempt to conquer all such struggles, we must first conquer ourselves.

We are not incapable of anything. Our only weakness exists in our strength, exists in our freedom, in our ability to choose what we want to achieve and make such things achievable.

08/08/09

(18+)

If you want something to become something else, treat it as if it already is (something else). You must become the change you wish to see.

15/08/09

The skies are as black as they get, allowing the stars and the lights on the boats to signal each other. Rain has begun to fall and the smell of the earth is wonderfully intoxicating. It's one of those nights when sleep remains a dream.

02/09/09

The imbalance still exists.

A large number of things continue to remain unclear, but clarity, I suppose, depends on how and from where you're viewing it.

13/09/09

Some days you awake filled with an immense amount of joy. Everything you hoped for has arrived, and the sun is shining its brightest and calling you to bask in its golden warmth. It asks you to stay, until your skin begins to burn and your eyes lose their purpose. Your body shrieks and writhes in pain, until you realise that what you believed to be true was not your reality.

15/09/09

I don't know what to do with you, and me, and everything we've been and are. I wish it were easy enough to put it all in a box and let it consume me as and when I please.

I think that's what I'll do.

28/09/09

If, a year ago, you told me that this is where I'd be, this is how I'd feel, and this is who I'd become a year later, I would probably have laughed.

Now I need so much more. It's a good thing I need you and not some Scandinavian dude. At least with you I'm comfortable enough to communicate freely.

30/09/09

I miss us, and everything we were and everything we could've been.

01/10/09

You're a closed chapter. I can't keep doing this to myself and I won't let you. It's important you know you're gone.

04/10/09

I always thought people had needs and looked to other people to fulfil these needs. I never thought I'd just need you.

06/10/09

(18+)

There are nights when I lie awake thinking of you. And I know that if I fall asleep, it will only be to dream of you. That is what you've become to me – a mere dream.

<u>09/10/09</u>

I like to think of myself as a constantly evolving idea.

I apologise for the extensiveness of this mail, and if you now think of your past self as being rather self-obsessed (which you probably do, while remembering that the adjective is quite appropriate). I must go now else this will go straight to your Junk mail.)

Remember to follow your own rhythm,

Much love,

Ruth.

Share Your Experiences

Wisdom Child

Email for Stories & letters: wisdomchild@live.co.uk

Thank you for reading these stories, we hope that it was enjoyable for you.

Tung Nguyen

Hello my name is Tung Nguyen. I was originally born in Hong Kong and came to England when I was 4. I am a student at Kingston University and am currently studying a degree in entrepreneurship and management. I have 3 A levels for Business, accounts and economics and also have a beginner's certificate in, NLP, Counselling and life coaching. I participated in many council events and meetings trying to tackle problems facing teenage crime and violence. I have organised many social events and invested in many new founding businesses such as SN media and Project Humour.

I started this project with the purpose of helping other teenagers to learn and reflect on their own Lives. However, after reading all of your own fantastic and heart warming stories, I ended up learning and reflecting on my own life. Thank you.

18+

I am very proud to have been involved as an author and thankful that we have received so many responses from our friends, family and supporters. I know that the book will be widely read and appreciated by all.

Everybody teenager has a story to tell, and may your stories be the first step that can enable other teenagers to live better and happier lives.

<u>Raheel Shah</u>

At present I am studying for BA (HONS) Entrepreneur ship and management, at Kingston University. Previously I was doing my IB Diploma in Ecole Mondiale World School, in Mumbai, India.

I have been involved in many organizations with a presence internationally. I was the founder and the president of an NGO called Red Ribbon Club. The NGO used to have public rallies and group discussion on the topic of HIV AIDS. We also fought for their rights against the society in total. I was a guest speaker in more 25 schools and 15 colleges around Mumbai on the topic of HIV AIDS, and involved in many inter school debates regarding the topic. I am currently referred to as a founder, trustee and alumni for Red Ribbon Club.

At the same time I had interest in films and acting and directing and I enjoyed watching Shakespearian plays as well

18+

as Guajarati plays from our community. I was the president of the filming club in my school, I have also directed many of Shakespeare's plays and acted in many, some of them being, The Tempest, The Merchant of Venice, The Midsummer Night's Dream and The Othello.

I was also involved in the Model United Nation, where I started off as the delegate and got promoted to being the Director of Human Rights, I also represented my school in Egypt at the American School Of Cairo for MUN were I earned the title of "Future Leader".

I have also worked in various pharmaceutical companies such as Virdev Intermediates, LYKABDR and MJChemPharm. I am also the Director of BDR Pharmaceuticals.

These was a little bit about me and my achievements so far, one of the reason why I got involved in this project of being an Author to this book is that I believed in it and believed that it would pass the message to the other teens that they are not the only ones who are suffering there others as well. The best part of this book is, it's not only us who have written our experiences, and we have approached teens globally to write in their experiences.

<u>Bar Segal</u>

I am 20 years old and currently residing in the United Kingdom. I was born in Israel until I was six when I moved to Budapest, Hungary. There I finished my twelve years of school and decided to study around the London area. I am currently in my second year at Kingston University. I am working on my Bachelors with Honours in Entrepreneurship and Management. Previously I attended the American International School of Budapest where I completed the International Baccalaureate.

I have worked and participated with many charity organizations. Starting with a dog shelter for stray and abandoned dogs where we helped clean the shelter inside and around. Then I helped sort out and pack clothes that were given in through charity drives for the homeless. I moved on to working and playing with wonderful children and teens who suffer from HIV in Constanta, Romania in a house called *Casa Speranta*. Following this I joined my school in a trip to

(18+)

Bosnia-Herzegovina to help pass out food, goods, and school material to families who were affected by the war in a few small towns. In the UK I worked on raising money for Cancer Research in a Valentine raffle sale.

I also have a passion for theatre arts, where I played in several school plays and directed one. I took diverse roles from main characters to side characters. Alongside this I have participated in the Model United Nations in Lisbon, Portugal representing Lebanon.

My family and friends helped me to get to where I am today, thank you. This book being a compilation of stories written by teenagers about life experiences and lessons learned allowed other teenagers to relate and realize they are not alone. Sometime we have personal problems that we don't want to share with people, and through this book we can see that other teenagers have passed the same obstacles of life. I truly hope it helps change lives for the better.

Loell Wolfries

I was born and raised in Kingston, Jamaica and moved to London at the age of 15. As you can imagine, life is a lot different in these two capitals and it is a privilege to have experienced living in both Jamaica and the UK.

I was a student at Campion College in Jamaica, Islington Arts and Media School (London), Woodhouse College (London) and currently I am at Kingston University (in London— a funny coincidence) reading BA (Hons) Entrepreneurship and Management.

I started my first business at 18 years old and ran it for a year—shows that you can really do something when you put your mind to it. I also work with Global Generation—a charity dedicated to working with the local community, businesses and young people on sustainability. Whether it's delivering workshops, hosting events or delivering corporate presentations, it's always a pleasure giving back to the community and helping others.

I've had a lot of exciting experiences growing up, especially as a teen when all the problems hit and the world just doesn't get it. It's weird the way your parents, teachers and coaches used to be teenagers but it seems like they just don't understand what you're dealing with at times. It sucks feeling like your problem is one in a million and that's why I was dedicated to being an author of 18+.

I hope that when you read this book you will find something you can relate to; I want you to see and understand that teenagers from all around the world face similar problems. Sometimes the stories themselves will not directly relate to you, but the concepts are very similar and you will definitely find something you like.

<u>Ronald Baguma</u>

I am currently studying three A levels which at Kingston university taking entrepreneurship and management. Before that I was at **rainbow international school Uganda** taking my A levels in Business Studies, Psychology and ICT.

In the past I was in charge of the finances for 'Habitat for Humanity'- which is an organization that builds houses for the homeless in Uganda. My duties included making sure we raised enough money to build the house, creating budgets and monitoring how the money was spent at the end of the school year. This was a very fulfilling task because not only was it appropriate to what I would like to be doing in the future but it was also an opportunity to give back to the community at the same time as giving to those who are less fortunate than myself. I underwent a work placement in both Year11 and Year12. In Year11 I worked as a sales person at a mobile phone shop which I valued as teaching me some public relations

18+

skills. In Year12 I worked at a car dealership where I observed and learned about various management techniques and skills required to manage a business.

Hopefully university will help gain the social skills which will equip me to become a citizen of the world. Growing up I have always had the love for business and making money thus my degree choice.

This book was made to let u know that there have been people in the situations u have been as well. You're not alone

Contributors

We would like to thank the anonymous contributors and the following people,

Zifeng Wei

Thomas

KG

Daniel Kaplansky

Dheer Shah

Gaargi Sharma

Ruth Pinto

Eric Janse

Tahira

18+